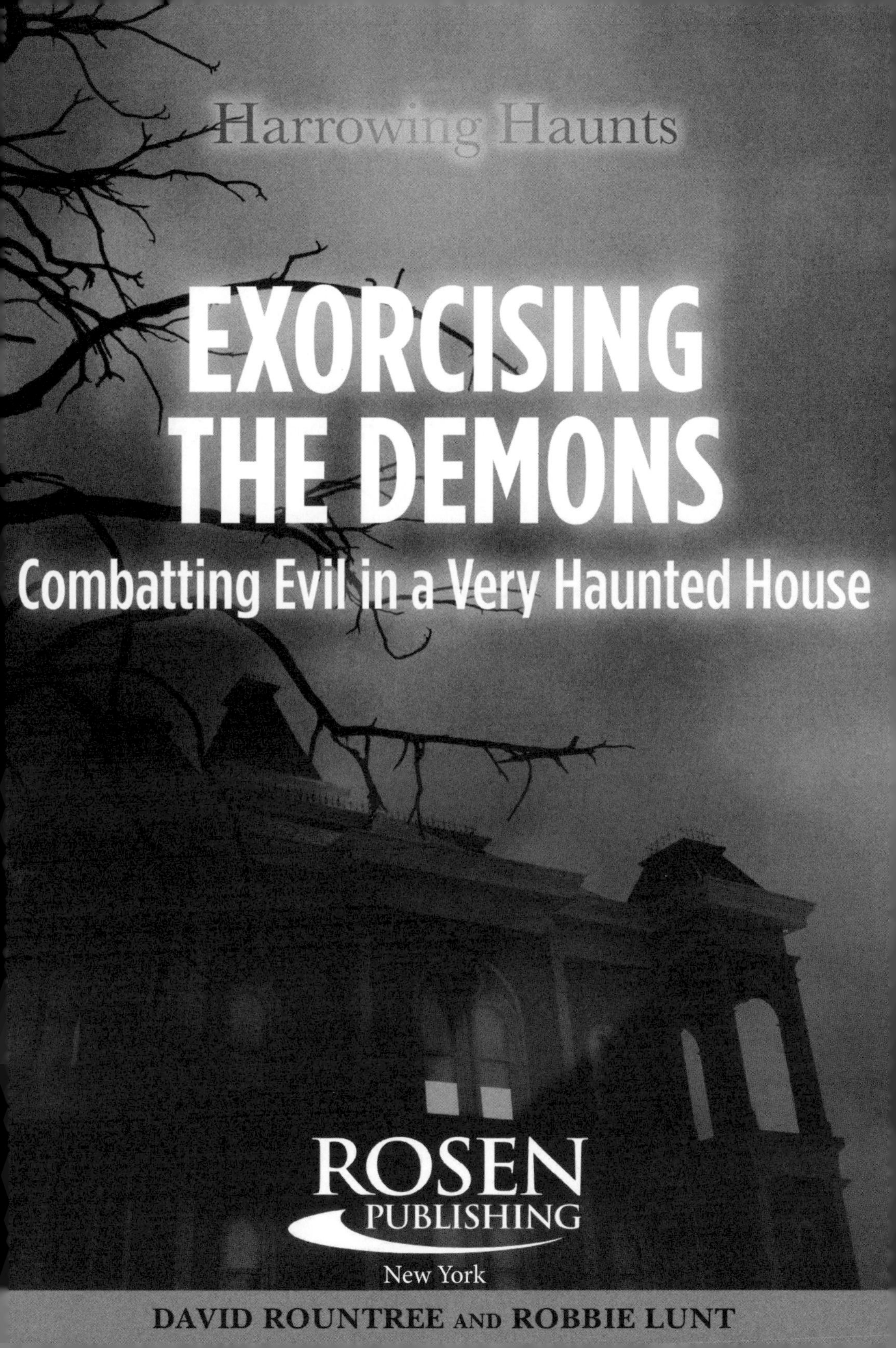

Harrowing Haunts

EXORCISING THE DEMONS

Combatting Evil in a Very Haunted House

ROSEN PUBLISHING
New York

DAVID ROUNTREE AND ROBBIE LUNT

This edition published in 2017 by:

The Rosen Publishing Group, Inc.
29 East 21st Street
New York, NY 10010

Library of Congress Cataloging-in-Publication Data

Names: Rountree, David M., author.
Title: Exorcising the demons : combatting evil in a very haunted house /
David Rountree and Robbie Lunt.
Description: New York : Rosen Publishing, 2017. | Series: Harrowing haunts |
Includes bibliographical references and index.
Identifiers: LCCN 2016010403 | ISBN 9781499463927 (library bound)
Subjects: LCSH: Demonology--United States. | Parapsychology--United States. |
Occultism--United States.
Classification: LCC BF1517.U6 R685 2016 | DDC 133.4/20973--dc23
LC record available at http://lccn.loc.gov/2016010403

Manufactured in China

The authors have reconstructed the dialogue and events in this book to the best of their collective memories. Any errors are entirely their own.

As well, names have been changed to protect the scared, the scarred, the innocent, and the guilty ones that were fooling around where they shouldn't have been!

Contents

Introduction

David

"Coyote is my power animal, an ally. He assists me in this world and the next. Your ally may not be Coyote. Umm...in fact yours may be Chimpanzee...."

In 1976 I began having strange dreams in which my deceased grandfather came to me and began telling me stories. He was teaching me lessons handed down to him from the Native American side of my family. One medium advised me to keep a journal. I needed to write down everything I remembered when I awoke each morning. She said my grandfather was preparing me to enter the spiritual life of my ancestors.

Later that summer, I moved from Mississippi, where I had emancipated myself from the Air Force, and relocated to Hawthorne, Florida. At the time, I began to study aspects of the paranormal from both a scientific and a metaphysical point of view. I found myself working in a shop for a man named Henry Lokison. Henry always considered himself to be a sorcerer. We would spend many days talking about the mysteries of magic and power. He introduced me to the writings of Carlos Castaneda. Though some people claim it was all a fabrication, I found truth and wisdom in the writings, in many cases some of the situations resembled stories from my grandfather. Armed with this confirmation of knowledge, I continued to practice the lessons I had been taught by my spiritual grandfather.

In the summer of 1978, I spent time in the Dakotas, searching for my identity. It was during this journey of self-discovery that I met a medicine man called Black Eagle or Wanblee Sapa, although it was Black Eagle who actually found me. Throughout the course of that summer I never left his side. He said he had talked to my grandfather and that he would bring everything together for me. Connect the dots, so to speak. I would go on a spirit journey, and I would get a native name.

By the time I left I was a fledgling medicine man, practicing Coyote Medicine, living in a world of wonder that simple words cannot explain. I began what was called "the quest for knowledge." Black Eagle said that in the quest for knowledge you need to be persistent as a dog. Though I thought that was funny at the time, I now know what he meant.

There are four steps on the path of knowledge.

The first step is the decision to become a medicine man. To do this requires many things, with the primary portion being an apprenticeship of sorts. During the course of the apprenticeship, the pupil changes his or her entire perception. After apprentices change their views about themselves and the world, they take the second step.

They become warriors. A warrior is a being of utmost discipline with control over himself. He learns to have unbending intent. It is by this unbending intent that the warrior unlocks the secrets of manipulating the world around him.

The third step, after acquiring forbearance and timing, the warrior becomes a medicine man.

When medicine men learn to see, they have taken the fourth step and become a seer. Seeing is not an affair to be accomplished by using the eyes; it is accomplished by using the heart.

Black Eagle warned me that once I embarked on this journey I could never turn back. He told me I would have to learn or be destroyed by the path.

I would learn. In time, I would pass on what I learned. I would have an apprentice.

And I would also forget. This story is about that experience and the result of "remembering."

Robbie

The first thing I can remember "wanting to be when I grow up" was a parapsychologist. I have always been very empathic. I had trouble playing the dozens because my insults would cut straight to the heart. I always knew where people's most vulnerable spot would be. That was just the half of it. On several occasions, I would dream of people who lived some distance away. These were unusual dreams, being very vivid and very clear. The next day the very people I had dreamed about would appear for an unexpected visit. On another occasion, my family went on a trip to visit Stonehenge; I couldn't believe I was the only one who could feel the ground throbbing. It was almost overwhelming. The rest of the family just kept on, not noticing a thing. It dawned on me that I was different.

Being an army brat, my family moved often. There were few constants in my life, so books became my solace. When I became interested in a subject I would devour it—every book on the subject I could find. Ghost stories and the arcane were of particular interest, whether fiction or nonfiction. I read *The Exorcist* when I was in sixth grade. Even at a tender young age I had read enough to realize the truths that were behind the story.

When I was 7 my father enrolled me in karate. We would begin each class with a meditation period. The sensei would also discuss chi. He emphasized how breathing is so important to cultivating that chi. I studied on and off with various teachers; through it all I always followed the spiritual side of the arts.

My work as a lighting guy carried me to many venues, from old theaters to municipal auditoriums and stadiums, many of which were haunted. In time, I worked a show with Dave and our friend Doug. The three of us hit it off; we all had the same twisted sense of humor—utterly dark. Doug mentioned that the Big House where he lived was for rent. It was a large, cross-shaped single-story house that sat in front of the little mother-in-law hut that he rented.

The big house had been empty for some time. There was a reason it had been empty for so long. They just didn't mention it before we moved in. I had remarked since I was young that I wanted to live in a haunted house. Be careful what you wish for. Spirit decided to give us a warm-up before the real fun began.

Together we will unfold a story that is incredible in scope and fascinating in content. We both will swear on a stack of Bibles that it's true.

Even if you choose not to believe it, it is a good story. So settle back, keep an open mind, but beware of men who claim they can conjure demons....

Chapter 1

The Beginning

David

I asked Black Eagle, "So what exactly is Coyote Medicine?"

He chuckled, "In being a medicine man, one has many paths open before him. What determines the path he walks is threefold; first of all, the Great Spirit guides our feet upon the path; then, animals choose us for their own reasons; and finally, power. Power selects; power chooses. We can only witness and go for the ride.

"To my ancestors, Coyote was the creator of the world. There is always hidden wisdom where Coyote is concerned. He is the source of an endless amount of knowledge. He is also a horrible trickster. Often his lessons are hard learned, riddled with failures and confusion, but then there is a lesson to be learned from that. He teaches wisdom as well as folly, and how to walk the balance between the two. It is only fitting that Coyote should choose you on your quest for an animal. Although I think a chimp would be more appropriate." He chuckled again.

"So you want to be a medicine man? You must think about this very carefully, for once you step down the path, there is no turning back. Once the door opens, it never closes. You like boxes that you can throw a switch and it hums. Well, there will be no switch—no turning off that hum on the path. And let me add that you will meet many enemies as you travel on the path. A defeat by any one of them means your personal annihilation. The path will never be without obstacles, from insurmountable blockages to sharp stones that rend a man's moccasins. You must give this much thought indeed. If you still want to learn, I will tell you what I know. It will take a while and require action on your part. You can't watch it on the squawk box that hums. You must learn the ways of our people."

He looked through me, clearing his throat. "A man rides forth to knowledge just as he rides into battle: wide awake, with fear, with respect, and with absolute certainty. In many ways, going to knowledge is going into battle. You will battle the world, as well as yourself." He tapped my chest over my heart. "Going to knowledge or going into battle in any other fashion is the action of a fool. Whoever practices this idiocy will live to regret his steps."

Black Eagle stopped for a moment, lost in thought. Then he broke the silence of the wind blowing across the Black Hills. "I am going to teach you the secrets that may make you a medicine man. You will have to make a very deep commitment because the training is long and arduous. You must endeavor to persevere; a medicine man is one who has followed the hardships of learning. I tell you he is a man who has, without rushing or without tripping over his feet, gone as far as he can in unraveling the secrets of power and knowledge. He is not just someone who cures a stomachache for a chicken and two eggs. To become a medicine man one must overcome the four enemies."

"I will become a medicine man. Who are the four enemies?"

Black Eagle chuckled, "Simmer down, Tonto. You can't eat the dog's head before you cook it. When a man begins to learn, his objectives are a low cloud, blinding him much like his head is stuck neck deep in a mud hole. His heart lacks meaning; his intent is without form, like a buffalo without a spine. I ate Jell-O once. It is like that. He dreams of many horses and of treasures that will never come to him for he lacks the knowledge of the path. But then, a remarkable thing begins to befall him. He slowly begins to learn, painfully, and in spite of himself. He crawls and claws his way toward knowledge bit by bit at first, then eventually he struggles to his feet, rushing toward it. But by then his thoughts begin to conflict with one another. The reality of what he learns is never what he pictured, or imagined, and he begins to be afraid."

I laughed. "I would never be that scared. I don't get scared anymore."

"You will, Tonto, you will. Learning is never what you expect. Every step of the way there is a new task. With each task the fear that you will feel will mount mercilessly, unyieldingly, until your entire purpose becomes that battlefield we talked about. And so you will have encountered the arrow bite of the first enemy: fear!"

"Why are you calling me Tonto?"

"Because you are a Squawk Box, injun...."

Robbie

May 1985

After spending the morning setting up lifts and trusses, and hanging and focusing lights, we had lots of time to burn. We were in White Springs, headwaters of the great and colorful Suwannee. Unfortunately, this year the state was suffering from an extended drought. The sun reflected blindingly off of the exposed white rocks that should have been the creek bed, making them resemble the twisted remains of some long-dead dragon. We sat in the shade watching the heat waves rippling up over the land as the tiny stream undulated onward in its journey to the sea. Penelope (Penny), wife of one of the crew (Norman), turned to me with a serious look on her face and said, "Can I tell you something?"

I should elaborate. For no particular reason, people, oftentimes complete strangers, will confide their deepest darkest secrets to me. That's not all; they will tell me things that they would never tell anyone else. Some of these things most people wouldn't believe. This was going to be one of those cases.

She proceeded to spin an incredible tale. "It's like this: Sometimes when I drift off to sleep, I become aware of a big eye. It's a huge, black single eye that grows larger and larger until I fall in and it completely envelops me. Then I'm pulled out of my body. I am suddenly in the presence of an old man with a beard who takes me over to the other two houses on the property where I live. The old man shows me the five ghosts that are on the property. There are three male spirits and two female spirits. One female is a young woman; the other one is much older. The older woman stays secluded in the bedroom closet in the main house."

Noticing that I was not looking at her horrified, or blowing her off as some loon, and was actually taking her seriously, she quickly continued, "There are constant noises in my house—noises that have started to get louder and louder. At first, I thought the squirrels or some other animal had gotten into the attic and were running daily marathons up there. But now I'm not so sure. The skittering has changed to banging with definite footsteps, human footsteps. It's really unnerving when I know I'm the only one home. To top it off, recently my son has befriended a new imaginary playmate. I look over at him and he's having these very real, animated conversations. He's looking intently at something that I can't see. It's obviously very real to him. Lately, things like cups, books, and jewelry have begun moving by themselves. I know where I put these things down. When I turn around they're somewhere else. Doors are opening and closing by themselves."

"What does Norm think about it all?"

"He doesn't see or hear anything. He thinks I'm losing my mind. He says it's all a bunch of nonsense. I have talked about moving but he won't hear of it."

Penny was scared, that much was certain. From what I had read about these things, what I had been exposed to, I could tell the house where she lived was definitely not a happy place. Her description of the big eye was very disconcerting. It really made me uneasy; it sounded demonic.

"Hey, I'm no expert," I interjected, "but if I were you, I would just move out. That eye thing just doesn't sound good, ya know? Think about it. If somehow Norman doesn't see the light and you think you need help give me a call. I might know someone who can help. But really...move!"

Earlier that month, my friend Dave and I were out in front of his apartment. It was dusk. Things just felt really weird. We were talking with his neighbor Carol. As we talked, Dave got more and more agitated. The creeping darkness didn't feel right, and I began to feel very uncomfortable. There was a subsonic buzz that just kept getting louder and louder. Some of the cicadas had managed to get into my skull. They were singing away. But you could feel it on the outside, too. Carol didn't seem to notice it at all.

Dave finally excused himself for a minute and went in to his place. Moments later he came out with an ornate bag full of colored corn. Indian corn, I think they call it. He said he was having a feud with someone in his neighborhood. He poured some of the kernels out. He did some hand passes over the corn while mumbling to himself. He then threw it to the northeast with a great amount of force and flair. I heard the weirdest howl, then these strange crackling noises. The buzzing immediately stopped, and the uncomfortable feeling dissipated.

Dave told me that he was a medicine man. He had just thrown sacred corn at his adversary. He raised his eyebrow when I told him what I had heard. He gave me the bag of the corn in case I should need it. I figured Dave would be able to help out. I made a mental note to tell him about Penny the next time I saw him.

Back at the concert, darkness had fallen; I had to get to work. Penny and I talked throughout the festival but her house didn't enter the conversation again. I finished the gig, and then continued on to a busy summer. I promptly forgot everything she told me. But I would be reminded soon enough.

Labor Day Weekend

I went over to hang out with my friend and mentor Samantha. In Florida, during the summer, if you live in an older house you keep it dark inside because it stays much cooler that way. Samantha was sitting in a pool of lamplight. The effect was somewhat dramatic. My eyes were first drawn there, but then I realized there was someone sitting back in the corner of the room in the shadows. When the woman leaned forward, I was startled by her disheveled appearance; I wasn't sure who it was. It dawned on me it was Penny!

There was something very, very wrong with her. She looked twice her age; the black circles under her eyes were entrenched deeply like unholy scars. Her hair looked as though the Addams Family's Grand Mama was her stylist. There was an uneasiness about her; she kept giving little furtive glances to the corners of the room expecting to see something. She seemed to be getting glimpses of things Samantha and I could not perceive.

Her husband had left for a video shoot halfway around the world in the Soviet Union. He was to be gone for at least five weeks. Trying to get any communication in or out from behind the iron curtain was nearly impossible. Norm was effectively out of the picture for some time to come. This left Penny at home, with her child and something abhorrent, alone. Whatever was manifesting there clearly understood her vulnerability. The spirits were capitalizing on it. The activity had ramped up. Her son's imaginary friend became scary and wicked in nature. She started to worry about his safety.

She said, "It was the last straw when I looked over and Michael was arguing with his imaginary friend. He was floating 6 inches off of the floor. I finally sent him to stay with my parents in Tallahassee. But now I'm all alone in the house."

She paused for a moment and then continued, "Robbie, it's every night. That eye. I close my eyes and there it is pulling me out of my body, always pulling me. Showing me things I don't want to see. Making me do things I don't want to do. It always takes me to the other apartment on the property, and to that old man. When I am awake, the noise and racket is constant. The scratching, the banging—it seems to never stop. When I'm in the kitchen, I can see a weird, twisted party happening on the balcony, complete with maniacal laughter and haughty carrying on, but I can't make out anything clear. I can hear a bunch of people constantly moving around. I can see their shadows through the shades but I sure am not going out there. I've moved into the downstairs room. When I need something from the kitchen or anywhere else upstairs, I run up as quickly as possible, grab what I need, and run back down the stairs to hide in the bedroom. I'm afraid to go to sleep and I'm afraid to stay awake."

It had finally gotten to be too much for her. The night before, she decided to sleep at the landlord's house. After the landlord and his girlfriend had gone to bed, Penny just lay there on the floor of living room, afraid to fall asleep. She heard a strange noise coming from the kitchen. It was a loud banging that made her catch her breath. When she got up the nerve, she turned her head to look in. What she saw, much to her horror, was the stove *dancing*. It was there doing a little Irish jig, hopping back and forth, all around. This was just the beginning. The true terror set in as she watched the hardwood floor on the far side of the living room bulge upward. A large wave the width of the room formed in the floor, and rolled straight for her. It threw her up in the air and continued on. When it hit the wall, it bounced back, lifting her, then letting her crash to the floor again as it returned to the other side of the room. She screamed, grabbed her purse, and ran out with what little she had with her.

She hadn't been back since. Samantha and I both worked hard to convince her to check into a hotel. We told her, no matter what, not to go back to that house.

I tried to console her: "I have a friend who might be willing to help you. I don't know what his schedule is, but I'm sure he would at least like to check it out."

"No one will be there this weekend. My landlord is out of town for the holiday. There are three buildings on the property. The main house is a bungalow. The other two buildings are cracker houses [a raised cottage–style home prevalent in the South] with a living area upstairs and a garage with a separate shop room downstairs. In my building, the one facing the school, the workshop has been turned into a small bedroom. That's the room where I'm staying. The center of the activity is the empty apartment above the landlord's workshop, in the house behind the main house. That's where the old man always takes me first, when he pulls me out of my body. Please, go by and take a look. I wish you could check out that other apartment. It's empty but you'll have to wait for my landlord, Clevis, to get back." She paused for a moment, remembering.

She added that a couple of years prior a 4-year-old in the neighborhood disappeared. They searched everywhere for her, but she vanished without a trace. Clevis just happened to go up into the apartment around dusk. When he went up there he found a very scared and confused little girl. She really couldn't explain how she had gotten in there. But she kept going on about the old man with the beard that had been there, waiting for her. So while the girl was returned unharmed (at least physically) to her parents, the event totally freaked Clevis out. Ever since then he'd kept the apartment locked up tight as a drum.

"When do you think he'll return?"

"Unfortunately he won't be back until Tuesday around noon, at the earliest. You know, though, if the house wants you to go in, it'll let you."

Sure it will....

Chapter 2

Labor Day

Black Eagle

Welcome to the world of your second enemy: clarity! Clarity of mind sends fear packing, but it will also blind both the eyes and the heart. It forces you to never doubt yourself. You believe you can do anything you want because you can see clearly into everything. You are brave because you are clear, and you stop at nothing because you are clear.

All of this is complete nonsense. It is indeed incomplete, only part of the grand puzzle. And if you should yield to this pretend power, you will be defeated by the second enemy. You will be patient when you should charge ahead, becoming befuddled, being incapable of learning anything. The second enemy has just stopped you cold. You will never be a medicine man. Your defeat will be utter, total, and final.

Robbie

"I saw Penny on Friday night. She was looking pretty scary."

"You mentioned her in passing. How's life treating her in the haunted house?"

"She had to move out. She tried to spend the night at her landlord's place on the same property. There was something about a dancing stove that drove her to a hotel."

"Wait—a dancing what?"

"Just the stove was in the kitchen boogie-ing away. It wasn't the stove really that drove her out; it was the floor tossing her around that really brought the point home. Would you like to go check the place out? There's not supposed to be anybody around this weekend."

The familiar throaty staccato of all the horses Dave had strapped under the hood of his big black van heralded his arrival. I stepped out into the yard just as the muscle machine pulled in.

"Taxi of Death?" Dave grinned.

I got in.

"Do we need to call Penny or anyone before we go over?" Dave was like a kid asking for candy in a candy store, as he slid the van into reverse and goosed the gas.

"Nah! The landlord is gone for the weekend. I think Samantha and I browbeat Penelope enough that she won't get anywhere near the place. We should have it all to ourselves. It's most unfortunate that we won't be able to get into the buildings until the landlord gets back."

Dave stood on the accelerator on 6th Street. I swear the sound of the engine had to have shattered some windows.

"It's a little loud, don't ya think?"

Nonplussed, Dave just turned the stereo up louder. "Better?"

We turned and headed east down the street. As we neared the target area, an approaching station wagon turned in front of us to pull into the driveway at the corner. Dave slammed on the brakes. I couldn't believe what I saw, as the van slide sideways to align itself perfectly with the driveway entrance.

"What? That looks like Penny."

"Well it sure isn't the Avon lady. I thought you guys talked her into staying away."

"I thought she was so scared that there wasn't gonna be any way she'd come back."

Penelope got out of her car and waved at us.

"Nice work, Robbie. Your ability to frighten either doesn't work, or apparently fear is not something she keeps in the front of her mind for long."

Dave straightened the van and parked on the side of the road in front of the house. We walked over the culvert into the yard; Dave noted I should pay attention to it. The ditch, with moving water in it, surrounded the entire property, like a barrier of sorts. Once we crossed the water, we were immediately hit with a feeling of extreme heaviness. Something just didn't feel quite right.

Old, tall pine trees were everywhere; there were also a couple of big oaks. A deep wall of foliage on the two sides of the property shielded them from the neighbors. The greenness of the light and the cloying feeling of the sticky humidity just added to the sense of malaise that crept up on you. Though it was hot, I got a shiver down my spine.

I walked up to Penelope. I was a little annoyed. "I didn't expect you to be here. Didn't you check into a hotel?"

"They told me you were coming. Two of you—you'd be here today."

A deep sense of unease passed through me.

"That's my place there." She pointed to the house on her left. "I figured it would be a good time to pick up some of my things. I sure wasn't gonna come over here by myself."

"Smart thinking," remarked Dave.

Her place was painted a faded dark green. Even in the sunlight it was foreboding. Two stories tall, with a closed garage door on the left side of the bottom floor and the front door in the middle. No windows on the first floor, but on the front of the second floor was a windowed balcony.

We stood outside as she recounted some of her experiences: "It just got to be too much. The noises were sporadic when they started, but now it's just constant. It's voices and footsteps."

The tension in the atmosphere was tangible. You could cut the air with a knife. It felt like the air might just cut back.

"I even tried to stay with my landlord, Clevis. But after the floor rolled me around like a wave in a lake I had to leave."

"So what exactly happened in your landlord's house?"

Penny recounted the complete dancing stove epic including the floor with the quantum wave. Dave listened intently to the whole story.

"Now which house is Clevis's?"

She pointed to the single story bungalow to her right by the road, "The other weird thing about that house is the back bedroom closet. There's the spirit of an old lady that lives in there. People who have rented the place have seen her. Clevis grew up here and sees her all the time. The door won't stay closed, you know? You can pile stuff up in front of the door, and when you come back the door is open. I can't show you because Clevis isn't here."

"Can we see the closet from the window?"

"Sure."

They made a beeline for the window to take a peek inside. I wandered by the old oak that stood outside the bedroom window. As I passed under the thick bottom limb, a vision froze me. The image was clear: a woman. From her I felt a horrified resignation. It was a place she had been before. From beyond my field of vision I could feel waves of anger and joy. I pulled away from the tree. I shook my head and tried to clear my mind.

"Hey, Dave. Come over here a sec, would ya?"

I had positioned myself so he would have to walk under the branch. As he approached me, he suddenly stopped dead in his tracks, right where I had my flash of insight.

"Someone died here, hung from this tree," he casually offered up this cordial tidbit. "I'm sure they died, then were buried at the foot here." He pointed to a spot that was particularly green and lush at the base.

We walked to the yard between the landlord's workshop and the main house. The workshop stood parallel to the bungalow; Pam's place was perpendicular to these houses. We did a quick once-over, scanning the area, taking it all in. The door up to the apartment was at the end of the building rather than the center. It had a ladder and buckets of assorted shop junk in front of it. The garage doors to the workshop were closed.

Penelope shook her head. "I know there's a watchdog in that workshop but he never makes a sound. I wouldn't want to mess with him, though."

We continued our tour to the space behind the two apartment buildings. It had once been a nice garden. Now it was a botany experiment gone awry. It was hemmed in on two sides by the garages. Two sides were dense shrubs and greenery. The neighbors could see nothing through those impenetrable walls. The garden part, however, was not doing too well. It was brown and dead, in complete contrast to everything around it. The weeds had not reclaimed the garden. That was odd.

We walked around the corner and entered Penelope's house. It was the smell that got you first. Bears smell fetid; road kill smells of death; food left to rot smells putrid. It was like all of those but worse. It was subtle—not really in your face, yet the smell was there. It was a palpable odor that invaded every nook and cranny.

We turned right, into the room she had been staying in. The place was a bedlam, the aftermath of a grenade attack on a baseball card store. She had tried to move as much of her stuff downstairs as she could, but debris was everywhere. The word of the day was *chaos*. It was a dark little space; the only light was what came through the door and a small table lamp. She had as many of her possessions stacked high on every open bit of space as she could possibly cram full. It was sadistically overflowing.

The activity upstairs scared her so badly she would no longer venture up there, even to eat. She wouldn't go on the front balcony, avoiding it like the plague. She had been inside her apartment on numerous occasions watching multitudes of people out on her balcony having a party—or, at least, people's shadows having a party. It was the kind of soirée she certainly wasn't interested in.

We went up the narrow, dark, wood-paneled staircase to the upper floor and encountered the same thing. I couldn't believe you could actually live in that kind of squalor. There were just piles in all the rooms forming paths to get where you needed to go. It was the same in the kitchen. There were stacks of dirty dishes heaped over the entire countertop. Empty and open food cartons jammed in the spaces among the dishes. Cockroaches had taken full control of the area; they were big and mean. Washing the dishes and putting things away would have meant staying upstairs longer than Penelope was capable of enduring.

She would do what she needed to do upstairs, get something accomplished, and then escape to the downstairs as quickly as possible just leaving whatever, wherever it was.

Dave just looked around and whistled. “Does there seem to be a center of activity?”

“At first not really. But now the front balcony is always busy.”

“What happens when you go out there?”

“I don’t go out there! There’s nothing! I keep the shades drawn because seeing the shadows is bad enough. I don’t want to see what’s causing them.”

“How long has it been since you’ve gone out on to the balcony?”

“At least a month.”

Of course, we just had to open the door and venture out. The stacks continued with the added attraction of a vertigo effect. It was very slight; the floor felt just on the verge of tipping over. The balcony wasn’t that wide to begin with. Now, with everything that was stored out here, the path was barely more than one person wide. There was no way anyone was getting on her balcony to mess with her head. Saying it was claustrophobic was quite the understatement. The balcony ran across the full front of the second story. There were about 12 sets of jalousie windows—some open, some closed, and some in-between.

“This is just the place where the stuff happens in my house. The real center of activity on the property is the other apartment above Clevis’s workshop. Every night when I go to sleep, when I get pulled from my body that’s the first place we go.”

“Is there anybody renting that apartment?”

“Oh no, Clevis wasn’t able to get anybody to stay in it for very long. He was living up there himself and renting the front house. But I guess people couldn’t stay there, either. There was a little girl that got lost. Clevis found her up in the apartment. It stays locked up after that.”

“Alive?”

“Yes, but she was messed up mentally I think after that.”

“I can imagine. Is there anything else?”

“Well, there is the bed. There are four ropes that always end up under the corners of the bed.”

"Okay—ropes. What do you mean?"

Penelope fidgeted about, obviously uncomfortable with the subject. "There are these four ropes that have loops on one end. No matter where they are put in the apartment, they always end up under the corners of the bed."

Penny was getting uncomfortable so she deftly changed the subject. "It's really gotten worse since Norm left on his trip. Nothing would happen when he was home. At least that's what he said. But when he left for work it would start up. They know he's gone for a longer time this time. The activity is now nonstop."

I really wasn't paying much attention to the conversation. It faded in and out; I was feeling a little strange. I could almost hear voices, but not really. I was out of balance. The edges of everything were fuzzy.

I looked down, and there was a large wolf spider crawling on my forearm. That wasn't hazy; he stood out perfectly clear, in sharp relief to the unreality around us. He was the size of a silver dollar. The thing was heading his way up toward my elbow. Severely arachnophobic as I am, that wasn't a big spider. No. To me, that was a monster spider. I didn't have a hissy fit and run screaming like I usually would have. I was calm; I just reached down and flicked it off. I never felt it crawling on me.

Penny and Dave continued their discourse; I looked up, noticing the window directly in front of me. Very slowly, and without the handle moving, the window was opening. I watched for a bit, just to make sure. When it was almost fully open, I interrupted my friends.

"Excuse me. Is this window opening or am I imaging things?"

Dave looked over, and just grinned and nodded.

Penelope exploded in a total frenzy. "It's them! Leave me alone. Just leave me alone!"

She grabbed the handle forcefully, spinning the window shut. She then went storming down the stairs and out of the house.

"Hold on." Dave turned. He pointed to the window Penelope had closed. "If the spirits of this place want to talk to us, they will open this window."

We followed Penelope into the sunshine. While she calmed down, we talked more about the things that had been occurring. Dave asked her some specific questions.

"Penelope, have you noticed anything unusual with odors?"

"Yes, it smells terrible all the time around here. I can clean up and it makes no difference. After a while I just stopped cleaning. It didn't matter."

"Do you hear voices?"

"I hear entire conversations. Sometimes I can make them out clearly, but other times it is just a drone."

"It would really help if we could check out the other apartment."

"We can walk around the outside but I'm pretty sure the door is the only way upstairs. Clevis is so paranoid about it; he keeps the key on his key ring in his pocket. It will be late tomorrow afternoon, if not Wednesday, before he gets back."

"Well, at least let's take a peek."

We walked over to the door to take a look. Through the dirty screen we saw the lock was unlocked and hanging open. There was a key in the lock.

"You gotta be kidding me!" I was floored.

"Gee, Penny, it looks like Clevis didn't have the only key," Dave chuckled as he grabbed the ladder and set it to the side.

As we quickly moved the buckets of bolts and scraps, I looked down to where they had been sitting. I realized the stuff had been there for some time. The dirt and debris were really built up around the door. The buckets were too heavy to move by themselves.

We pulled open the screen to make sure our eyes weren't playing tricks. There it was, unlocked. The apartment had been padlocked shut. The door handle hadn't been turned at all. The hasp was still closed. The lock was just hanging open.

"This just isn't possible. Clevis has been obsessive with keeping people out of there. He would have never left the key in the lock," Penelope exclaimed.

I removed the key and gave it the once-over. It was rusty and covered with dirt. "I don't think this key was in your landlord's pocket."

Dave took the key and examined it closely. “It looks like someone dug this up from the yard. It doesn’t feel right, either.”

“Just so we could go in and take a peek. Isn’t that special.”

Dave looked at Penelope, “Are you going to give us a tour?”

“No, no. I think you guys will be fine. I’ll sit out here in the nice, bright sunshine.”

I decided to put the lock in my pocket while we looked around. Why take chances? I sure wouldn’t want to be locked in any place on this property, particularly this apartment. Call me superstitious, but I ain’t crazy.

As we climbed the stairs Penelope called up to remind Dave, “Look in the bedroom; it’s to your right. See if the ropes are under the corners of the bed.”

The first thing I noticed when we got upstairs was that the walls throbbed. You could feel the walls breathe. Everything seemed to have a green tinge to it, that weird, sickly, day-glow kind of green. The stairway leading up had been bright, but once you got into the apartment it was appreciably darker. It was open and claustrophobic at the same time. We slowly looked around. The apartment was sparsely furnished but not used. It looked like someone lived there but had left quite a while ago. They didn’t move out, they just left—like the Mary Celeste, frozen in time. We went to the bedroom. There was an annoying feeling of abandonment. The shades were half drawn. The ropes were there under the four corners of the bed at the bedposts. We had obviously entered a shifted reality. However, it didn’t feel as though anything was there, just a weird old house. So we went back down the stairs.

Penelope looked at us expectantly as we came out of the door. “So, how was that? Interesting?”

Dave shrugged his shoulders. “It was trippy, but just weird. Nobody was home; nothing really manifested.”

I agreed. “It was just a really creepy, peculiar-feeling place.”

“Really, I expected you to get a show.” She sounded disappointed. “If I go in with you it’ll be different.”

“Penny, you don’t have to do that.”

"No, Robbie. I want you two to see what I've been going through and believe me. I'm sure it will be different."

She got that right. The energy increased dramatically as we returned—definitely stronger, and a whole lot weirder. It was a potential energy, a mysterious tension. The house was holding its breath, trying to decide whether to relax or explode. When we got to the top of the stairs, Dave and Penny went one way; I went the other. The walls shimmered with sickly green iridescence. The light coming through the windows was grayed down—a cacophony of greens and grays. Unlike Penny's house, it just smelled musty. That or my olfactory nerves had finally become inured to the smell.

The big, open living/dining room was darker than just a few minutes before. The shadows in the corners were deeper. They slowly moved when you watched them out of the corners of your eye. I went into the kitchen. It was brighter because of all the white, but it was still dingy. The other door in the kitchen led down into the bathroom.

I've seen sunken rooms but never a sunken bathroom. The kitchen, the hall, and a bedroom each had a door that opened to a set of stairs down into the bathroom. I walked around to the hall door. I noticed a bizarre pattern on the floor. The finish of the hard wood was worn away. I closed the door, standing where the wear marks were. There was a small peephole in the door looking right down at the toilet. Intrigued, I went back into the kitchen. There was the wear pattern there. The peephole from the kitchen overlooked the whole bathroom.

"Hey guys, you've got to check this out."

They walked over to the kitchen.

"This is pretty creepy, but in an Uncle Ernie kind of way. Come—look at the door."

Penelope peered into the bathroom, "Eww!"

"I found one at the hall door, too. I haven't checked the bedroom yet."

As Penny and Dave headed there, I cut through the bathroom to meet them. It felt like walking down the stairs into an abandoned pool. The feeling of despair in the bathroom was almost too much to take. It felt black in there even though it was the middle of the day with the sun shining. It was a horrible place—oppressive.

It made you want to cry.

Dave opened the door to the bedroom, “There’s a peephole here, too. And a magazine collection I think you’ll like. I don’t know if I’d take any, though. Something might get jealous.”

The oppressiveness of the bathroom eased enough for me to continue to the bedroom. Nothing was happening, yet it felt like the heart of a maelstrom. I closed the door behind me; I saw the third identical spot. The view was right into the bathtub. The other two were by the bed looking at the pile of magazines.

We all turned to the closet of the bedroom. We walked to the door peering up. The closet had a trap to the attic that was open, but you could see nothing. It sucked light like a black hole. You couldn’t look up there very long. It started to pull at you in a repulsive way.

Dave took a step back, his attention riveted to that discomforting void. “Whoa, I’m not quite sure what that is but it’s a strong one. It may be a vortex or possibly a portal of some kind.”

“The old man has shown me this spot when he pulls me from my body. This is where all the spirits come and go. Come to think of it, none of them that I saw ever seemed really nice.”

The outside wall of the closet didn’t look right. It had strange paint flecks that formed a kind of palm tree pattern. It was a pillar with a kind of “poof” or mushroom on top. It was shaped like an umbrella. We looked closer to discover it wasn’t flecked paint; it was embedded hair—fine black hair.

The feelings struck me at once—the anger, the malice—and it was overwhelming. The poor victim slammed against the wall, hand tight around her throat. Ground up the wall to the full length of an arm. Then shaken like a bulldog’s prey, pushed harder and harder against the wall. We all realized what we were looking at.

Penelope shuddered, the scene disagreeing with what little sanity still dwelled within her. “I’ve never seen that before. I can’t stay in here any longer. I have to go.”

She hurried out as fast as possible. Dave and I took our time as we walked out of the bedroom. He took the ropes from the corners of the bed and tied them to the door handle as we walked out.

"I have to see this for myself, Robbie. I mean, moving ropes, dancing stoves, wavy floors—the paranormal circus has come to town."

We walked downstairs and put everything back where it had been. We even put the lock back with the rusty key still in it. We found a nice spot of sunlight to stand in. It was bright and welcomingly warm—a stark contrast to where we had just been.

"You guys really need to meet Clevis. All these ghosts are his. This has been his family's house since it was built."

"Clevis, eh? I would really like to meet him. He seems like an interesting guy. What do you think, Robbie?"

"That sounds like a fun time."

"Cool. So, Penelope, when he gets back call us. We would be happy to drop by for a chat."

We walked back to Penelope's house to get her purse so we could leave. When we rounded the corner our gaze was drawn up to the balcony. To our shock and amazement, every window on the balcony except the one Penelope had closed, was wide open. Dave and I froze in our tracks.

I turned, stunned. "Are they trying to tell us something?"

"I don't think they like us anymore, Robbie," he snickered.

Penelope quickly stepped in the door and grabbed her purse. She was shaking and even paler, if that were possible. "I need to leave. Now! I really don't feel that comfortable. I will call you on Wednesday and let you know what Clevis says."

Dave and I walked back to the van. As we walked off the property the sun got brighter; life seemed better. The low buzzing that had started when we walked on to the land finally abated.

"Did you notice that?" I took a deep breath. "All of sudden a huge weight has been lifted off my shoulders. The farther away we get the better I feel."

"I'm happy to be back in the light myself," Dave looked at me and grinned. "I saw the spider. That was interesting you didn't scream like a little girl. Was it truly a spider or do you think it was something else? Nudge, nudge; wink, wink."

When we got home Dave and I told my girlfriend, Leigh, what we had been up to. We both agreed it would be a lot of "fun" to see if we could help out Penelope. After we had been at my house for about an hour the phone rang. Penny called to inform us that her landlord would be showing up at around 7 p.m. that evening. He was very interested in meeting us. Apparently, he was coming home early.

My only question was: why?

Chapter 3

Labor Day Evening

Black Eagle

Once you defeat your fear, you may turn into a buoyant warrior, or just a clown, or perhaps a jackass. But your clarity, which has cost you so much, will never change to fear again. You will be clear as long as you live, but your path will have ended. You must do what you did with fear. You must take a stand against clarity and use it only to see. You must wait and judge carefully before taking new steps. You must believe, above all, that clarity is almost a mistake. Then a moment will come when you will understand that clarity was only a point before your eyes.

At this precise moment you will have overcome the second enemy, and will arrive at a place where nothing can ever harm you again. This will not be a mistake. It will not be only a point before your eyes. This will be true power. You will then know that the power you have been seeking for so long is yours. You will truly be able to do what you please. And it is now that you have come across the third enemy: POWER!

Dave

I couldn't believe what happened that day. Robbie brought me into contact with a woman, who I was almost certain had a demon influencing her home and her life. I was fairly certain that her landlord, Clevis, was behind it. And what kind of name was Clevis?

When we left Penelope's house earlier, I had driven my friend Robbie home. We hung out talking to his girlfriend about our experiences that day. They both knew Penelope well, but I was at something of a disadvantage, having just met her once before in a casual circumstance. According to Leigh and Robbie, Penelope's mental health and general condition had degraded significantly over the summer.

It had been a heck of a summer. I had to travel up to Virginia and bury my father. It was an unexpected blow that impacted me a great deal. But Labor Day changed it all. With Penelope's phone call—that strained voice—we decided to pile back in my van so we could head over to the property. The landlord had made an unexpected early return.

Coincidence?

I have learned that there is no such thing as coincidence. This situation would prove to be no different. I climbed into the van, fired up the engine, floored the accelerator, and appreciated the G-Force of 500 horses galloping at once.

Robbie

I climbed into the van to head back to Penelope's. Dave and I turned to each other and at the same time said, "Wonder why they cut their trip short?"

We broke out in laughter.

When we arrived at the property, Penelope was already there waiting with Clevis, the landlord, and his girlfriend, a mousy-looking girl with glasses. Clevis certainly was a sight. He was wearing coveralls, a beat-up old fedora, and scruffy brogan work boots, and had big chunk of chew in his cheek. He reminded Dave and me of a classic north Florida redneck from the 1930s. As we entered the property, the same heaviness prevailed upon us once again. It was physically hard to breath.

Penelope introduced us. We started discussing the problems Penny had been having. Clevis just laughed.

"Oh, there are lots of spirits on this property. They're here to help me, and they're also my protectors."

"Well, who is the old man with the beard that Penelope keeps telling us about?" Dave asked. "It sure ain't the Fuller Brush Man."

"No, that's my grandfather. He built this place after he moved here from Levy County."

"The old lady in your closet that Penelope told us a little about—who the heck is that?"

"I don't know; never really asked. It's always been that way since I was young. Darn closet door will not stay shut. It don't matter what you do. Pile stuff in front of it or what have you—it just won't stay closed. I have tried rehanging the door, but it don't make a bit of difference. Once in a while when you walk into the room you can even see her standing there all calm an' such, looking out of the bedroom window just as pretty as you please. Just like she was as alive as you an' me." He chuckled. "And that stove—it's always made noises in the middle of the night, even when it was still a wood burner. We never really paid much attention to it. Just the spirits playing around, I reckon."

"There was this one time: I was renting the house to a bunch of frat boys an' living in the back apartment. It was really late one night when I hear a big ruckus in the yard. I look out the window an' all them boys are runnin' out of the house in their Dr. Denton's like the devil hisself was on their heels. Yelling an' going on about the stove dancing an' I don't know what all. I guess that was the last straw, cause they moved out the next day—never even asked for their rent back. That was pretty funny. It's just the way things have always been round here. I'm sure all the stories are true."

"Is the front house there the center of activity, or is it Penelope's house?"

"It's neither of them, really." He spat a black stream of tobacco juice. "The power resides in the back apartment, the one above my workshop. That's where the energy is the strongest. We've never been able to rent it for very long. I don't know why. I never had a problem when I'm staying there. Would y'all like to see it?"

Dave grinned, and winked at Clevis. "We got to see it today."

"No, I mean I'll take y'all up there, show y'all inside."

I piped up. "We went in and looked around already."

"There's only one key for that lock. An' it's right here...." He fumbled around in his pocket and pulled out a big ring full of keys. He flipped through the keys mumbling to himself, "Ha! Here it is. I knew I didn't lose it. No way I'd want anybody wanderin' around up there."

Dave shrugged his shoulders and smiled. "That may be so, but we have been up there nonetheless. I took the four ropes and tied them to the door handle."

"Yeah, what about all that hair embedded in the wall?" I added.

Clevis looked at me like I was crazy. "What?"

"That trail of hair on the closet door that looks like an umbrella, but the hair is embedded in the paint."

"I've lived here my whole life."

Dave laughed. Penelope nodded in agreement.

"No. We saw it, too."

"Y'all are flat wrong I was raised in these houses. I've never seen anything like that. I grew up here; I know every inch of this place."

Dave nudged me and flashed his Checkered Demon grin. I knew Dave was setting Clevis up for something.

"Well, come on Clevis, we'll show you. I believe you may have missed an inch or two."

Dave seemed to be enjoying Clevis's uncertainty.

While we had been talking, twilight had slowly sneaked past us, and true night was descending.

Dave took the opportunity to walk away. "Hold on a sec while I run to the van."

Penelope climbed onto the tailgate of the pickup that was parked between the workshop and the house. She sat there with Clevis's girlfriend.

She spoke to no one in particular, "I'm sure as heck not going in there, not this late."

Dave came trotting back with a flashlight. We walked over to the apartment; Dave shined his Maglite at the door that led up the stairs to the second floor. Sure enough, just as we had described, the key was still in the lock. It was unlocked.

Clevis was dumbfounded; Dave was thoroughly enjoying it. "That's not right. I *know* there was only one key. I made sure there was only one. I need to see what y'all are talking about with that paint. This ain't right, I tell ya."

Dave and I moved the buckets along with the rest of the assorted stuff from the door. Everything was right where we had returned it to earlier. We opened the screen door and Dave pointed the light at the door handle.

"Wait. That ain't gonna work. Hold on." Clevis headed to the door of his workshop. "Lemme get something."

He swung open the door, and we all blinked against the bright light. When I focused, I saw lying on top of the back workbench a huge jet-black chow. It didn't bark. It didn't even growl. It just turned its head, staring at us with soulless, piercing eyes. It was glowing with malice. I could feel the quiet invitation to come in. Probably not the best idea...

Clevis came out of the workshop with an old hurricane lantern. "Spirits don't like electric light—spooks them. They are more active around a natural flame."

He closed the workshop doors. The only light in the courtyard was a few distant streetlights and the light that bled out from the bungalow. He deftly lit the lantern as we moved to the door.

Dave turned back to the women. "Are you sure you girls don't want to go with us?"

"You boys just go and have a fun time. We'll just stay here and hold down the fort."

Clevis pulled the key from the lock and looked at it. It was rusty and had bits of sand in the grooves. He was mystified.

"Really I was sure...," he mumbled. "We had a problem with this little girl."

"I understand. Penelope told us," Dave reassured him. He looked at me sideways with a grin.

Shrugging his shoulders, Clevis hung the lock on the hasp. He and Dave started up the stairs. I hesitated for a second while I grabbed the lock. I put it in my pocket. Better safe than sorry and a lock that somehow unlocked itself may be able to lock itself—just saying. I had no intention of being locked in the upstairs of that house for a minute. When I walked through the door it swung shut on me, hitting me hard.

I had to push it open again. Then I headed up the stairs. That was a bit unnerving.

When I got to the top of the stairs, Dave and Clevis had already gone into the bedroom. They had found the ropes under the mattress corners.

Dave was just shaking his head in amazement. "I left those tied to the door handle. I also tied some serious knots in the ropes. They're all undone."

Now it was Clevis's turn to smile in the gloomy semi-darkness. As the glow from the lantern faded into the bedroom, they disappeared from my view. The living room took on a new personality. It glimmered in the surreal green color that Dave and I had witnessed earlier. It wasn't so much a fog; everything was glowing in the dark. I mean everything, from carpet to floors to ceiling. It made it fairly easy to see around; the light emanated from everywhere at once. The walls were really moving in and out, expanding and contracting. The house was panting—in anticipation? It was incredible! Mesmerizing!

Facing the stairs in the middle of the living room was a big-armed easy chair, there was a man sitting in it. He wasn't a flesh and blood man, because I could partially see through him. He was green, too. The green guy sitting in the chair just looked at me, smiling, creeping me out. Dave had smiled, Clevis had smiled, now this ghost man smiled, so—what the heck—I smiled sheepishly back. I noted that the guys had moved over to the fun closet. I hurriedly made my way to them.

When I walked in Clevis was leaning over to the wall, bringing the lantern up close while he and Dave examined the hairs. "Wow. I've never..." He didn't quite finish his sentence, as a blood-curdling scream ripped through the air, chilling me to the bone!

"They've got her! They've got her!" Penelope was shrieking hysterically.

In a flash, Dave and Clevis went blowing by me like a twister on steroids. They ran down the stairs with the only source of light among us, leaving me alone, upstairs in that greenish glowing netherworld. My legs tried to unlock themselves from the floor. With my feet spinning, I quickly turned to scurry after them.

The door was half shut when I got to the bottom of the stairs. I opened it and ran right into a wall—not a physical wall, but that's the only way to describe it. The air was so thick I was stopped dead in my tracks. I pushed through as hard as I could. I was fighting through the air to get out of that house! When I finally battled my way across the threshold of the door, I almost fell over as the pressure released. I exploded out into the night; the bubble popped, letting me make good my escape. I was disoriented momentarily; I had to shake my head. The courtyard felt almost normal when I got my breath, except for the fact that I appeared to be alone. The back door of the main house was open; it looked like everyone had gone in there. I ran up the three steps to the little landing and tried to cross the threshold. I hit that thick air feeling. Running in molasses, I had to push my way through. Again, the bubble popped to let me pass.

Everyone was in the living room. Clevis's girlfriend was sitting in a chair in the corner just staring out into space, not moving at all. She was an absolute blank. Checked out—into the great-wide open—la la land—missing—lights on, but no one at home.

Dave was questioning Clevis when I walked in: "Aren't you worried about your girlfriend?"

"No need to be. She does this all the time. She'll be fine in a few minutes. They always do this to her."

"Really?" Dave, annoyed with Clevis, turned to Penelope. "What happened? What made you scream like that?"

"We were just sitting at the truck when Bobbie-Jo reached over and grabbed my wrist really hard. She started to dig her nails in. It hurt really bad. When I looked over she was staring down. She slowly turned her face to me. I swear her smile went ear to ear and was all teeth—sharp, insane teeth. Scared me." Penelope showed us by trying to duplicate the smile herself. It was scary. "When I screamed I threw her hand off. She got that blank look on her face. I dragged her in here and sat her in that chair. She hasn't moved since."

Dave dragged Clevis over to make sure she was okay. As they approached she got the strange, twisted, inhuman toothy grin again. There was nothing in the gaze, however, as that remained an empty, vacant look. They backed off to the other side of the room, standing over by the bookshelves.

"She's possessed," Dave said rather innocuously.

I looked around. The bookshelves in the room stood out as they lined the walls and were packed. Books weren't the only residents. There were old scrolls, parchments, ancient-looking vellum, papyrus, and leather-bound manuscripts that had the aura of age. I happened to notice an especially worn and battered version of the *Necronomicon*, bound in leather.

The *Necronomicon* is a reportedly fictional grimoire made famous by writer H.P. Lovecraft. Written supposedly by the "Mad Arab" Abdul Alhazred, it is quoted in several of Lovecraft's and other horror writers' stories. It features what has been termed the "eldritch entities." Among other things, the work contains an account of the "Old Ones," their history, and the means for summoning them. However, I would point out that it clearly states that there are no known banishments for these entities. So although it may be a fictional work, this particular copy looked very real to me, all bound up in ancient leather. In fact, unless it was my overactive imagination, this particular copy seemed to exude a certain horror around it. I also harbor the belief that any incantation recited with strong intent has the potential to summon something. But this was not the only brow-raiser on those shelves. There were tons of books on sorcery and witchcraft, all obviously well read and all obviously extremely aged.

"Wow, Clevis. You are quite the reading man, aren't you?" Dave began reading the titles from the old books: "*The Clavicule of Solomon, The Lemegeton, The Book of St Cyprian, The Book of Sacred Magic of Abra-Melin the Mage, Pow-Wows, The Magus, Malleus Daemonum, The Book of the Law, The Book of Lies.*" Dave whistled and slowly shook his head. "Impressive. These books are worth a fortune just for their age value, much less their content."

I kept expecting the stove to start dancing.

"My grandfather started the collection. I've been able to add to it here an' there. University town people get interested in subjects an' then move on. They get rid of treasures they don't even know they got."

The conversation faded into the distance. Something was pulling me to the back bedroom. I could feel it nagging at me. "Hey, come back here," it seemed to be beckoning me. "We're having fun back in here." We needed to check it out.

I tugged on Dave's shirttail like an errant child. "Hey, guys. We should check out the lady in the closet."

"Stop tugging and check it out yourself, Robbie."

Clevis nodded. "Go ahead if you want to."

I decided to just do it myself. I went into the hall outside the bedroom. The first thing I noticed was it was incredibly uncomfortable. My skin felt like it was crawling with insects. Also, something was daring me to open the door. I had an unbearable desire to do so, yet cold, dark fear wouldn't let me. Wave after wave of bone-numbing terror rocked my body senseless. No matter what I did, I could not get myself to open that door. Finally, in frustration I went back.

"Y'all really need to check this out. Something's going on back here."

Dave looked at me and a shadow of concern crossed his face. "Are you okay, Robbie? You are white as a sheet!"

"You should really feel this."

The four of us walked into the little hallway (really a little connector hub more than a hallway) and headed toward the infamous bedroom. We left Clevis's girlfriend propped in her chair taking a mental vacation. As everyone reached the bedroom door there was a collective "whoa!" We hesitated; the energy hit everyone fairly hard. We all looked at each other as Clevis opened the door. I was still expecting the stove to come dancing out among us.

As we entered, Clevis looked to his left and said, "That's just not right. That closet door is never closed."

"Seems like a lot of firsts for you today, eh Clevis?"

He ignored Dave's barb. We all stood in front of the door in wonder. Good old Dave—he had a suggestion. It made my blood freeze when he opened his mouth. "Robbie, why don't you walk over there and open that door?"

I'm still not exactly sure what happened. Maybe it was latent ninja survival skills? I walked over and opened the door, and there was a howling blast. Next thing I knew, I was standing behind Dave and Clevis about 5 feet away from the closet. How I went through them, I will never know. I was just there.

As Penelope slowly crept closer to the open closet, she peeped up into the top shelf area. She began to prattle on and on: "There's something up there. What's up there? Do you see it? What is it? What is that?"

She leaned forward, staring into the darkness intently. She then screamed and slammed the door shut, freaking out!

"Penelope, are you okay? What did you see?" Dave asked.

"I saw these two little red dots. I realized they were two glowing red eyes. When I realized that, they started coming at me. I freaked out; it scared the heck out of me. Can we leave this room, please? Like right this minute. This place is freaking me out!"

It wasn't doing me any good, either, to be honest. Dave, of course, just chuckled. So did Clevis. (Great—they both shared the same sick sense of humor. This was going to be a long night.)

A lifetime later when we returned to the living room, Clevis's girlfriend was still there in the chair. But instead of the thousand-yard stare, she was rocking back and forth, quietly sobbing.

Clevis, indifferently unconcerned, offered up a thin reassurance. "Don't mind Bobbie-Jo. She'll be fine in a minute."

Penelope had apparently reached her limit, "That's all I can handle. Could someone please come with me over to my house? I need to grab some things before I take off."

Being a friend and also feeling the need to vacate the presence of Clevis, Bobbie-Jo, and their house o' fun, I decided to go with her. At least she wouldn't have to go into her apartment alone. When we entered, I noticed the place was vibrating. You could feel everything just humming. There was a conversation going on right below a person's ability to make out what was being said, just a constant murmuring. We went upstairs, Penelope made sure to keep her gaze down at the floor. She only looked up long enough to locate what she was searching for. She was scared.

On the other hand, I was not so smart. A multitude of shadows was moving out on her balcony. Back and forth they mingled, sometimes three deep. They must have cleared away the stacks of boxes and furniture, judging from the movement. A regular party seemed to be going on out there, but because I didn't have an invitation I decided not to crash it. We quickly vacated the upstairs.

We grabbed the last few things from the downstairs room and we loaded them into the car. I took Penelope's keys and locked her door tight.

I tossed back her keys. "Goodnight, Penelope. Try and get some sleep. I'll let you know what's up."

In the yard, Clevis and Dave had been locking up everything and talking between themselves (God knows what about). After Penny drove away, they came over to where I was. Clevis walked right up to me, real close, face-to-face.

"I can conjure demons. Can you?"

"I don't want to conjure demons."

"That's not what I asked. I asked if you can conjure demons. I can." He held up his right hand. "Grab my hand."

I am still not sure why I did what I did. Dave told me it was because I had a date with power. I swear that Clevis knew exactly where he was in his yard. When I grabbed his hand and looked at him, his face went dark; just a tight rectangle of light lit up his eyes. It looked just like the lighting effect the Hollywood vampire always has on his eyes when he's hypnotizing people. He knew where to stand to get that effect from a street light; I'm sure he did. But I didn't have time to think it through.

I felt a huge surge of energy rushing out of his hand heading down my arm. My whole arm was being enveloped by a thick, numbing pain. The flow made it to my bicep by the time I was able to concentrate my chi and fixate on it. Clevis's power was fast but I stopped the energy cold. The depths of my mind were screaming—running in fear! I kept a calm demeanor, and I still maintained eye contact.

A strange look crossed his continence, and then it quickly passed. "What did you see?"

"I didn't see anything."

"Normally when I do that with someone they see my face go through 11 or 12 changes. I'll look like someone completely different. You didn't see anything?"

"Nope, didn't see nuthin'."

He dropped my hand and stepped back, mumbling, "They always see some changes."

"Robbie is not an average person, Clevis," Dave stated. "He is learning to be a shaman."

"A who?"

"Like an Indian medicine man."

"Really?"

"Yes, so he is learning to handle power. So he won't see your projections. He sees only your energy, your power."

"Oh, I see. Well, everyone else sees my face go through changes."

"I have no doubt that they do."

"I can conjure. My grandfather taught me that. I can do other things, too."

"I believe you."

While Dave and Clevis were talking, I began to look around.

It started occasionally, and then picked up in frequency. I began to notice shadows on the side of Clevis's house. It looked like all kinds of people kept running through the yard, yet there was no one there—no one physically, at least.

"Hey, do y'all see all the shadows on the house over there?"

Dave was now being particularly guarded about what he said around Clevis. He just looked over and nodded.

"It happens round here now an' then. It's just my friends."

"Friends, eh?" Dave remarked.

"Yeah, they're my guardians."

After one very pronounced set of shadows ran by, we even ran around the house from both sides just to make sure nothing was going on. We checked that nobody was messing with us, but still we saw no one.

As we continued to talk I started to hear children laughing. It was somewhere in the neighborhood of 11 p.m. on a school night; the little children should have been long in bed by then. But these weren't normal children. I kept hearing them. These children would never need sleep again.

Thinking I may have lost my last vestiges of lucidity, I broke into the conversation. “I…uh…realize it’s kinda silly, I know, but are y’all hearing little kids giggling?”

Dave grinned. “Yeah it’s been going on for a while now. I was waiting for you to notice it.”

Clevis just laughed uncontrollably.

We wandered about the yard in conversation. The stroll had ended up in Penelope’s driveway, talking about some of the books Clevis had. The quiet murmuring of children was disturbed by a violent *WHAM!!* It erupted at the top of the staircase in Penelope’s apartment. Then it came again—*WHAM!!* The whole house shook. But this one was at the base of the stairs. I locked the door myself; I know there was no one in the place. I am absolutely certain I was the last one in there.

It sounded like two people started at opposite ends of the staircase, and then walked up and down the stairs slapping the wall with flat axe handles. Clevis just looked at us and broke into an unholy smile. The whole ground was shaking to the beat of those ax handles; all the windows were rattling. The house seemed to come alive. The cacophony kept up for about a minute and forever or so. It rose to such a din that I thought the cops would show up.

Then the whole property went dead quiet. I mean *dead* quiet. Even the constant buzzing in the brain ceased. Dave looked at me and I looked at him.

I couldn’t resist. “You know, Dave, on that note it’s probably time to go.”

“You’re right. Clevis, it was interesting. Thanks for the tour.” He still had that grin on his face.

“Feel free to come back anytime. We’d be happy to show you what y’all want to know.”

The flood of relief we felt when we left the property was eerie.

Dave

We drove away from Clevis’s property discussing everything that had happened. I was particularly interested in two distinct events that had occurred with Robbie—one was the closet incident; the other was the encounter with Clevis in the yard.

"What I want to know, Robbie, is what you saw up on the top shelf of that closet."

"Well, that's just it. It was like I was hit by a blast of air, to the point that my hair blew back like that Maxell commercial. I saw what looked like a glowing ball of fuzzy light up on the shelf. It felt like an old woman."

"Of course, it was an old woman. But I am more impressed with how you went through Clevis and I without knocking us out of the way. It's like you moved through us."

"I'm not sure how I did that. Suddenly I was just there."

"Ah...you may have actually experienced the double. One more thing: When Clevis grabbed your hand, what did you see?"

"A scary redneck with delusions of grandeur?"

"Good."

Chapter 4

The Fellowship of the Crystal

Black Eagle

A man defeated by power surely dies in a fog. Power is, after all, the supreme burden. He will have no command over himself, and doesn't have a clue when or how to use the power he holds. In effect, his power is useless, feeding on him like coyotes feed on putrid flesh.

If you lose to any one of these enemies there is nothing you can do. You will have lost utterly and completely. Once you give up the ghost you are finished. But if you are only blinded by power, and you turn your back to it, the battle is not lost. You are still actively trying to become a medicine man. You will be defeated when you no longer try. It is then you will realize that the power that you believed you conquered is in reality never yours at all.

You must hold yourself in check, handling carefully and faithfully all that has been revealed to you. You will come to see that clarity and power, without control, is a mistake. You will see that everything must be held in balance. Then you will know beyond a shadow of a doubt when and how to use power. You will have defeated the third enemy. By this time, if you are still among the living, you will near the end of your journey to knowledge. You will come upon the last of the enemies: old age!

Robbie

The phone rang, smashing the silence like an axe.

"Hey, Robbie. It's Dave. Funny thing happened a minute ago. I took my wallet from my pocket and a small slip of paper fell out. I didn't recognize the paper but it had a phone number on it. I hadn't put it in my wallet. I think we have a member for our team."

"Who'd that be?"

"Gwen. Her number is on the paper. I have no idea what the number is doing in my wallet. I haven't seen her in years. It is no coincidence it fell to the floor."

"Do you think she will help?"

"I believe she will. I intend to call her tonight. I need to speak with her as soon as possible."

"So what is Gwen in all of this?"

"Well, Gwen is an ex-girlfriend of mine. But better than that, she's a very powerful witch. She will help us, but I am just not sure how yet. One thing is for certain: I have to show you a lot of things very quickly. You are going to have to pay attention like never before. Once you start down this path there is no turning back. If you fail, you will die. Power has implicated you in this, so I have no choice but to try and show you the ways of a medicine man. That is all I can show you, but it will have to be enough. Gwen has land that will help in teaching you things you need to know. Meanwhile, pay particularly close attention to your home and what is going on around you. We are dealing with a demon here. After seeing Clevis's bookshelves, I am certain that he is responsible for whatever it is, and for it being here."

"Yeah, I did notice a dog-eared copy of the *Necronomicon* on the shelf. You seemed to be rather impressed with some of the other books."

"They are worth a fortune as collector's items, just for the value of the books alone. It's what is between the covers, though, that has me concerned. Clevis owns a copy of nearly every major grimoire I have ever heard of. And a few I haven't."

Dave

It was midnight by the time I dialed Gwen's number. It rang three times before she picked it up.

"Who is this?" She sounded a little annoyed.

"David," I replied. "Sorry to be calling you so late, but something rather weird has come up."

I quickly gave her the rundown on everything that had happened from Penelope's perspective and our own.

"We are going to need some help, Gwen. Are you in?"

"Well, I am not sure what I can do, but I would like to see the place for myself if you don't mind."

"Then I am assuming you are in?"

"Yes."

"Good. Now I am also going to need to bring Robbie out to your property. I need a place where he can become accessible to power."

"Call before you come."

"You're a peach, Gwen."

"Why do I get the feeling I am going to regret this?"

After I hung up the phone I thought about everything that had happened. It had been one heck of a day. My main concern was Robbie. He was not prepared to deal with what I suspected we would be dealing with. I wasn't sure if I was prepared to deal with it. I would have to work on exposing him to the knowledge I had learned. I needed some help in doing that.

I was sure I could rely on Henry. He had power, but in my opinion it was undisciplined. Still, he could be a help. He could also be a hindrance. I would have to keep an eye on him; his involvement would have to be closely supervised. Help in these matters is where you can find it. Henry was many things, but he was loyal to a fault.

It was late. However, I knew that he was a night owl. He didn't have a phone, so I figured I would drive over to his trailer, see what he was up to, maybe mention the day's activities. I drove by his home; of course he was up. I went in and we talked for about an hour. I told him the bare minimum details of the story. I asked him if he would be interested in helping me train Robbie in the ways of a shaman. Henry jumped at the chance. I told him that we would be coming by at some point to tell him everything that we were involved with. I would have Robbie with me; I felt Robbie needed to be accessible to power. Henry understood what I meant and smiled.

"You should take him to the Millhopper," he said knowingly.

"Oh, I plan to. I have a few other places that I plan to take him, but what is important is what you have in store for him when he visits you here."

The Devil's Millhopper is a very strange, powerful place. Just outside of Gainesville in Florida's sandy terrain and numerous pine forests, it's a round chimney-shaped sinkhole formed from a cavern collapse that took place about 10 thousand years ago. It is 120 feet deep with a wooden walkway that descends to a miniature rainforest. Small streams trickle down the steep slopes of the limestone sinkhole, disappearing through crevices in the ground, feeding the great Florida aquifer. Lush vegetation thrives in the shade of the walls even in dry summers. A significant geological formation, the Devil's Millhopper is a National Natural Landmark that has been visited by the curious since the early 1880s. Researchers have learned a great deal about Florida's natural history by studying fossil shark teeth, marine shells, and the fossilized remains of extinct land animals found in the sink.

One of the earliest stories about this hole comes from Timucuan legends regarding a princess that a demon wanted to marry; she ended up being swallowed by the hole. Another tale, supposedly from the 1880s, is about a black pioneer family on their way to town with a wagonload of cotton when they saw the hole open up and gobble down an acre of tall pines. It would be on Robbie's itinerary, a place where he could gather power.

There were other places that I felt would be significant areas to take him. Oak Ridge Cemetery, for example, on the way to Micanopy was another place I was particularly fond of. Oak Ridge Cemetery is the second-oldest graveyard in Alachua County. Its historical claim to fame is that it contains the grave and monumental marker for Madison Starke Perry, Florida's fourth governor, who served from 1857 to 1861. But there is another gravestone that is far more interesting.

Payne's Prairie, now a state preserve, is another place of power I planned to take Robbie. This large flat marshy plain embraces more than 20,000 acres of pristine wildness. Named after King Payne, a Seminole chief, it was once the home of Timucuan tribes. It then became a large Spanish cattle ranch in the 16th century. From 1871 to 1892, when the Alachua Sink was clogged, it became Alachua Lake. Naturalist William Bartram visited the prairie in 1774 to write about its wonders. I had been out on the prairie myself on numerous occasions at night and can attest to the activity there. The truth is there was no shortage of areas around Gainesville in which one could expose someone to the ways of power along with the energies of the earth.

When I got home, there was a message from Penelope on my answering machine. "David, they told me that you were going to help me. They told me all about you. I have some things they told me to tell you. Can I talk to you? Please call me."

She left her phone number. It was three in the morning; I decided this was a chore for me to tackle after I got some sleep. But sleep was something I would be getting very little of in the days ahead.

The buzzing alarm clock rudely disturbed my fitful rest, spurring me to hurl the pillow at the offending sound, knocking the clock effectively into the wall—the third clock fatality in as many weeks. Grumbling to myself, I staggered out of bed and headed for the kitchen to start brewing the coffee. A quick check of the refrigerator showed breakfast would be out of the question, so I decided to make a cup of coffee and head out to Skeeter's for an "Asher Special," a popular breakfast in Gainesville, regardless of the time of day.

My thoughts of breakfast were interrupted by the ringing phone. It was, of course, Penelope. She wanted to meet to chat with me about this Council she had spoken of. So to kill two birds with one stone, I told her to meet me at Skeeter's in half an hour.

I walked into the restaurant, scanning the crowd. It didn't take long to spot Penelope in a booth drinking coffee and fidgeting. Her hair was a flare on a dark, moonless night.

Penelope had huge dark circles under her eyes from lack of sleep and the stress she was dealing with as a byproduct of the activity at her house. She wore no makeup and it looked like she had slept in her clothes; she was just a wreck. I felt bad for her.

"They come to me in my dreams," she began.

"Who comes to you?" I asked.

"The Council. There are twelve of them, and they tell me things. Well, actually only one of them talks to me, but they all communicate with each other. He is the facilitator."

"Does he have a name?"

"Ranar. His name is Ranar."

"That is an odd name, Penelope. What do they look like?"

"It is hard to tell exactly. I mean, I sense them more than see them. They are shadowy. Ranar, though, is dressed in natural clothing, like furs and leather garments. He wears feathers, too. I feel like they may be Indians."

"You mean like Native American Indians? Their dress would seem to indicate that to me."

"Yes, I think so," she replied.

"There is a slight issue I have with this, though," I added. "Ranar is not a Native American name. It is an Indian name, all right, but from India. It's a very common Indian name."

"They didn't look like they were from India to me. They look very tribal. They tell me that they are here to help me, but they can't directly intervene. They can advise me, and they can help protect me, but they can't physically take on this thing. But they tell me you and Robbie can. There will be others helping you.... Ranar says others will come, and that others will help. It will take a lot of work. You will get help from unexpected places to remove the threat of this entity."

"Interesting. Is there anything else?"

"Only that you and I have something special between us. I am not sure what it is but I have felt that there is something we have to do, or something we will do in this. Ranar says you will teach me things—show me things that will help me." Penelope suddenly stood up. "I have to go. I am staying at the Sunshine Inn. Room 6. You can call me there. I have your number."

The Sunshine Inn. How ironic.

After she walked out, I finished my breakfast, wondering what in the world Robbie had gotten me into.

I hadn't been home five minutes when the phone rang. It was Penelope. I knew it before I picked up the phone.

"Hi, Penelope. Did you forget something?"

"You are supposed to teach me."

"Teach you what?"

"Ranar says you are supposed to teach me about power."

"Penelope, I am already teaching Robbie. I am also working on putting some people together to take care of your house. I am not sure how I am supposed to teach you, when power must point you out to me in order for me to teach you."

"Can you come by my motel room?"

"All right. I will be there in a little bit."

The Sunshine Inn was on NW 13th Street, not too far from Robbie's house, but across town from where I was living. It was about a 20-minute drive from my house. When I got there, I went straight to Penelope's room and knocked on the door. She answered the door after the third knock. She looked even more disheveled than the last time I saw her.

"Clevis told me he didn't want you guys to come over there anymore and disturb his guardians."

"Lovely. Any more good news?"

"The Council came to see me. Ranar says you are going to teach me things."

"What kind of things?"

"You are going to help me gain power. We are going to be together."

"I think maybe you should visit Henry and talk with him."

"I want to talk with you."

"Okay. What do you want to know?"

"I want to know why this is centered on me and my son."

"You are probably just a target of opportunity. Clevis needed a target; you were handy."

"Why did he need a target?"

"He is working a very special kind of magic."

It was late when I got to Henry's trailer. "Bad news, Hank. Clevis has put the lid on us visiting the property any further. He told Penelope that we were disturbing his guardians. However we handle this, it will have to be from afar. It stinks, but I have faith that we will get to go back at some point, so if the chance breaks, be ready to jump on it at a moment's notice. Gwen hasn't been able to see the place yet, either."

"Sure, just come get me. It's not like I am busy. How are your teachings going with Robbie? Is he learning? Have you given him the books?"

Henry was an avid disciple of Carlos Castaneda. Not just an avid disciple, but an obsessed one as well. All we talked about now when I visited him was Don Juan this and Carlos that. But Henry was like that. He was the same way about Tolkien's Trilogy when he was reading that. It became his life. The Castaneda books were even more so, as he seemed to gain power from reading them.

"He is reading the books, but he is also being trained in the ways in which I was trained in. Robbie has a background in Eastern philosophy and martial arts; he needs to get a more tribal approach. So I am teaching him medicine, but I am also teaching him to be a warrior—a warrior of the light.

"I think tomorrow's the time to sit down with Penelope and get the whole story about how this all began. I need to know everything I can if I am going to discover the true nature of this entity. It's no ghost, I can tell you that. I suspect it is a demon of some kind. There are just too many things that scream demonic to me."

Chapter 5

Clevis

Black Eagle

Of all the enemies a medicine man faces, old age is perhaps the cruelest of all, the one that he will never be able to beat completely. At best he can only struggle to keep it at a distance for a time. But you eventually reach the point in your life where you have endeavored to persevere. Your fears will have long fled back to the shadows from which they came, and you will have no more impatient clarity of mind. Your heart will see clearly. You will be patient like a rock that waits for the rain to turn it to dust. All your power will be balanced, in check, but you will also have a never-ending urge to just lie down, wrap up in a blanket, eat, and sleep.

If you give in to this desire, if you slip into the tiredness, you will have lost the last round. You will be a decrepit old man who pees his pants. Your need to rest will banish all your clarity, your power, and your knowledge. You will become an even bigger fool than you are right now.

But if you shake it off, sidestep it, live your fate through, you will be a great medicine man, a man of incalculable knowledge and ability. When you have beaten the four enemies, there are no mistakes for which you will have to answer. Your acts lose the blundering quality of an idiot if you can hang on. If you fail, or suffer a defeat after you conquer the four enemies, you will have lost only a battle. You will have no regrets, for you will shoot your bow again on another day.

Robbie

Penelope came over to the house that afternoon. Dave showed up shortly afterward. We all began to discuss Clevis.

Dave said, "I know you told Robbie some of this, but when did things start to get real bad? The place was already haunted, but something must have triggered the upswing in activity."

She told us that it all started when Clevis had convinced her and a friend to help him perform a ritual that would allow him to talk to his dead grandfather. She said they went to a remote clearing on forest service land in Levy County. Clevis told her it was his grandfather's place. As night fell, they built a bonfire. Clevis started reading from an old, battered, ornate leather-bound book. The wind picked up; it started to howl. When they had been at this for a bit, the other boy with them became violently ill and started to throw up. What was strange was that he proceeded to hurl for four continuous hours, nonstop. He finally quit when they had returned to Gainesville.

Dave gazed intently at Penny and said, "I need you to think really hard. Start from the beginning and try to remember the details."

Penelope thought carefully for a few minutes then restarted her story: "It started after the night that Clevis asked me if I would like to take a ride. I asked him why he wanted me to ride into the country with him. He confessed that he wanted to try a magic ritual that would allow him to talk to his dead grandfather. Newcombe—he's a mutual friend of Clevis and me—agreed to help him. I decided to tag along as well, because I was curious. We all piled in the truck and left town, heading west on highway 24."

She paused for a second to gather her thoughts, and then continued, "The sun was beating down on the hood of the car as we drove deep into farm country. After a while Clevis turned off the main highway and headed down a secondary road that had no street sign or route sign on it. We eventually reached forest service land, somewhere out in the middle of Levy County. I have no earthly idea where we were. Clevis turned down an isolated washboard road, again unmarked, and drove out through all those tree farms that are growing lumber for the paper mills and the plywood factories. I remember vividly how the smell of the pines mixed with the smell of the dirt as we kicked up a plume of dust driving in that secluded area. After several minutes of this, we broke free of the farms and into a rather beautiful hammock. There were ancient, massive, live oaks lining the dirt road, their branches hanging over, creating a welcome shade from the glaring sun. Long tendrils of Spanish moss were hanging everywhere, swaying hypnotically in the gentle breeze. It was an awesome day in the woods."

David interrupted her at this point. "Do you think you could find this place again if someone took you out?"

"No way. I had no idea where I was at that point and was a little worried. In fact, if Newcombe hadn't been there, I would have been terrified."

"Okay. Then what happened?"

"Well, we drove up to a clearing, where the road ended. There was a place for Clevis to turn around and park his truck. We all got out and stretched our legs. In the middle of the clearing was a large, well-used fire pit. A stack of wood was neatly piled up to the side of it, all ready to fuel a flame. It was obvious that this trip had been planned. You could also tell that many fires had been burned in the pit. Clevis then told us that this had been his grandfather's land years ago. He said that he came to this spot a lot. It had been a favorite place for his grandfather, too."

"Did it dawn on you that you may have made a mistake coming out there with Clevis at this point?"

"I was a little concerned, yes. But everything seemed okay. He was my landlord and friend."

Dave rolled his eyes. "Friend—sure he was. That's why his stove dances for you. Okay…"

"Well, Clevis grabbed a bag from the back of his truck and moved to the center of the clearing. He told Newcombe to start a fire. As he went to work, Clevis built a little table using some sawhorses and planks. From his bag he pulled out a book. There were about a dozen small sacks and baggies. As he laid the bags out neatly on the table, he told us the book was called the *Necronomicon*. It was full of spells and rituals used since the times of the ancient Sumerians.

"In those days there were Magi who used the rituals to raise and talk to spirits of the dead. He said that history was filled with examples of books having spells for this type of thing.

"He said that Odysseus, under the tutelage of Circe, a powerful sorceress in Greek times, made a voyage to the Underworld. It was an effort to raise the spirits of the deceased using the spells Circe had taught him from a book like the *Necronomicon*. He also told us that famous wizards, called Necromancers, had used these very same rituals to talk to the dead."

Dave interrupted once again. "He was telling you the truth at least. I find it fascinating that he used the *Necronomicon*. I had always thought that it was a complete work of fiction. But after seeing the copy he had in his library, along with the contents of that library, I have to give that thought some pause. The legend is that there are no known banishments for the entities conjured in that book. Are you certain that this was the book he used?"

"Oh, I am certain," Penelope replied. "That's the name he called the book. It was a very old, leather-bound volume, and the words were handwritten on a vellum type of paper."

"Interesting. Please continue."

"Well, by then, the sun set and the darkness took over. The guys built up the fire. The shadows started to dance—spirits on the canopy that cloaked the clearing from the night sky. Clevis lit a few candles so I guess he could see the table and read from his book. In the gaps between the overhead branches you could see that the sky above was dark—full of stars."

"He pulled a big knife out of his bag. It scared me! Then he used it to draw a huge circle on the ground. The circle was completely around the fire pit and the table and us. He made sure after it was drawn to let us know that under no circumstance were we to leave the circle. It would ruin the whole ritual. The other ramifications might not be too fun, either. He then took a bag of white powder—looked like sugar or salt—and poured it around the same circle."

Penelope dug a little deeper in her memories, pausing again to make sure everything was clear. "Well, then he started jabbering about opening gates. He was calling names I had never heard of, like "I call on Anu, Enki, Inanna." I had no idea what he was babbling about, and I think I was starting to feel real spacey.

"Well, we were standing around the fire, every few minutes Clevis would hand something out of one of the baggies to either Newcombe or me. He told us told to hold it for a moment, then put our "essence" in it and throw it into the fire. I am not really sure what it was we held, but sometimes it would spit and sizzle, and sometimes there were big flashes."

"Did you realize you were performing a summoning?"

"I had no idea what we were doing. Up to that point I guess Clevis had been praying or something like that—"blah, blah, please hear me" kinda of stuff. But then he began chanting in a language I have never heard before, really loud and forcefully.

"Of course, it was at that point that the weather took an abrupt turn for the worse. I remember looking up. I was no longer able to see any stars through the branches. It seemed like they had disappeared and only darkness remained. The wind picked up from a light breeze to a tempest of epic proportions. The trees around us weren't welcoming and beautiful anymore. The limbs were reaching into the clearing, closing in on us, like monsters of bark and leaves, threatening to swallow us whole! The Spanish moss came to life—Medusa's hair, snaking and striking among the branches shaking above us. Weird, though: Our hair was mussed up by the winds, but Clevis's baggies and his ritual things were untouched. The fire pit wasn't disturbed by the wind at all."

Remembering that tidbit gave her pause, but only for a moment. "Okay, then there was a blinding flash and a crackling explosion as lighting struck somewhere in the woods nearby. It lit up the forest with an eerie blue-white light. The wind picked up with the intensity of the chanting, blowing near-hurricane force at this point. When the next flash of electricity lit up the sky, I looked up, and all that met the eye were rolling, boiling black clouds. Lightning was landing all around us now, popping everywhere. The thunder shook everything. The air was filled with electricity that you could feel on your skin, your hair—the world was electric. The wind screamed through the trees in an unearthly shriek of sounds that made you cringe, like fingernails across a blackboard. As hard as it was blowing, it couldn't drive away the pervasive smell of ozone!"

She was getting a wild look in her eyes. "Clevis kept the invocation going, getting as frenzied as the storm, his face becoming maniacal with intent. There was a particularly loud boom, causing Newcombe to lose his cookies, puking in technicolor. No rain had started yet but the wind wailed, and the thunder and lightning kept pounding. Poor Newcombe just kept barfing, over and over again, nonstop. I have no idea where it was all coming from. Then Clevis stopped abruptly, blew out the candles, and then started to pack up his bags. He had a strange look on his face, an eerie glow that was enhanced by the play of the firelight. It was inhuman looking to me. Frightening."

"Then what?"

Penelope hesitated. "After power puking several times you'd have thought Newcombe would have been reduced to dry heaves. Amazingly, he just kept throwing up, repeatedly. I couldn't believe how much he was still spewing. The storm raged on but there was still no rain. The only moisture hitting the ground was coming from the poor boy hurling by the fire. And get this: Clevis wasn't concerned in the slightest. We waited for the fire to burn down, all the while Newcombe puking in time to the thunder. When it got to a point that Clevis could easily douse the embers, we were able to leave.

"Newcombe rode down the road with his head out the window. He was still able to wretch out fetid liquid like some organic volcano. I was expecting to see his guts come out any time.

"As we hit the first stretch of asphalt I looked up into the sky through the window and saw stars everywhere. There was no wind, no storm—just poor Newcombe heaving his entrails. He kept it up all the way back to Gainesville. When we got home I wanted to take him to the hospital. You just can't throw up like that for hours and have it be good for you, but Clevis would have none of it. It was just a reaction to the psychic power of the incantation, he told us; he would be all right."

"That is some reaction," Dave commented. "And it isn't normal."

"Well, that's the week that I started to see the big black eye in my dreams. It began that very next night; right after Clevis's grandfather came to me in a dream. Once he took me out of my body that first time to walk around my house and the back garden, all the other activity increased exponentially."

“I have no doubt that Clevis conjured his demon that night. What is affecting you came into this world as a result of that ritual,” Dave added seriously.

“Robbie,” Dave looked at me. “I think we need to do some historical research on Clevis’s grandfather. Can you do some digging at the library?”

“Yeah. I can go by there tomorrow.”

Chapter 6

Histories and Mysteries

Black Eagle

There are so many different paths. How will I know which path to take?

All paths, no matter how difficult or simple are the same: The scenery may be different, but in the end, they lead nowhere. They lead to nothing. You must take the path with heart. The problem is most people never ask the question; when it dawns on you that your path is without heart, the path is ready to kill you. By then, very few can pause to consider and leave the path.

A path without heart is miserable. Every step along it is a chore. A warrior, on the other hand, has no choice but to take the path with heart. A path with heart is light and free; it requires no effort to enjoy it. Still, remember, it is not the path: It is how you walk it. So in this vein, heart is everything.

Our people believe that you see the world through your heart. It is attached to the eyes. I have mentioned that choosing a path requires freedom from fear and ambition. Do not confuse ambition, however, with the desire to learn. It is our destiny as men to want to know everything. The path without heart will kill you. Remember that. It doesn't take much to die. In fact, dying is easy. If you are seeking death, you are seeking nothing. The challenge is to live.

David

The whole Sumerian connection that was developing was fascinating to me. As a student of history, I had read everything I could get my hands on about the Sumerians and found them to be something of an enigma.

Archeologists have placed the first settlement in southern Mesopotamia. It was called Eridu. Interestingly, the people of Sumer believed that their civilization had been brought to Earth, fully formed, to the city of Eridu by their god Enki. Mysteriously, the Sumerians had a language, culture, and appearance far different from their Semitic neighbors and successors. They were at one time believed to have been invaders, but the archaeological record has indicated that there was cultural continuity of several thousand years.

The term *Sumerian* applies to speakers of the Sumerian language. Sumerian is generally regarded as a language isolated in linguistics because it belongs to no known language family.

Sumerian religion has its roots in the worship of nature, such as the wind and water. The ancient sages of Sumer found it necessary to bring order to what they didn't understand. This delivered them to the natural conclusion that greater forces were at work. The forces of nature were originally worshipped as themselves. However, over time, a human form became associated with those elements. Gods in human form were then seen to have control over nature.

The gods of Sumeria were human in form and maintained human traits. They ate, drank, married, and fought among each other. Even though the gods were omniscient and all-powerful, it was apparent that they could be hurt, even killed.

With such twists and turns, how could you know if you were summoning a benevolent spirit or a wrathful god? The question remained of what were we dealing with—or, rather, whom?

Robbie

For most people the tedium of research would be daunting. Me, I love digging into books. Keeping my focus is more of a problem. I pick up a volume of an encyclopedia and find myself not only reading about the subject at hand but every other interesting tidbit in that volume. I read the dictionary, too.

Being a transplant to the Sunshine State, I only knew the general history. The state has had many flags fly over its soil: French, Spanish, English, Confederate, and American. Some of the earliest colonies on the continent were at Pensacola and St. Augustine. Early native Florida tribes, the Timucuan and Calusa, were decimated by disease and raiding. The void was filled by mostly the Creek and Miccosukee Tribe, whose members were pushed south by the continuing colonial expansion. The new tribe, who came to be known as the Seminoles, also assimilated the black slaves that had escaped to the southern wilderness. The expansion of the European and subsequent American population did not venture far into the southern expanses of Florida; the interior of the state was fairly hostile to the white man. Once "La Florida" was bestowed to America by Spain in 1821, a plantation culture expanded in north Florida. There were many wars fought with the Seminoles during this tumultuous period. Several of the battles were fought in the Gainesville area.

Florida sided with the Confederacy in the Civil War. The largest battle in Florida, the Battle of Olustee, happened north of Lake City near the Georgia line. During the same month there also occurred the battle of Gainesville. It was more of a skirmish than a pitched battle. Shots were fired; injury incurred.

After the war, Gainesville became a shipping center for cotton and other produce heading to the markets north. Although it was a commerce center, Gainesville was a frontier city through the 1920s. Like the Wild West, everyone carried guns and shots were often heard. Throughout the whole period of Reconstruction and well into the 20th century, justice was handed out by vigilante groups. More often than not, these were law-abiding "citizens groups." Lynching was common and not always racially motivated. Punishments often occurred for what they determined were moral indiscretions. When Gainesville incorporated, one of the first laws passed banned the use of firearms inside the city limits. The opening of the University of Florida mitigated some of the wildness but not much.

Levy County, where Clevis's grandfather came from, was a different story. What histories I could find, focused mostly on Cedar Key. Cedar Key is certainly an important part of the history, but there's so much more to it. The county is bordered on three sides by water: the Withlacoochee, the Suwannee, and the gulf coast. There are more than 200 springs in the county. All that water pouring from the earth creates deep green forests smelling of pine, magnolia, and dogwood.

Clevis's grandfather appeared to be one of the largest land owners in the county, yet in any of the histories he was never mentioned. The histories I could find consisted of things like bound and collected oral histories or *The Old Days of Levy County* by the Ladies Hysterical Society. They seemed to have something to say about everyone who was anyone. Yet, there seemed to be something missing. They were whitewashed histories following the great Southern tradition of not talking about something makes it go away. It just didn't make sense.

Clevis's house in Gainesville had no clear title that I could dig up. His grandfather had owned the land when it was rural. One interesting thing: There was a roller-skating rink right across the street. The neighbors had been complaining about the loud parties there for years. Of course, when the police would finally show up, the place would be shut up tight. It had been closed for a while yet the parties still continued. In asking some of the older Gainesville residents I knew, I discovered the place never really caught on. It was always a little eerie in there.

Dave said another part of our team needed to be Henry. He owned a repair shop where Dave and my neighbor Doug had worked. Henry had some interest in the metaphysical and considered himself a wizard.

We stopped by to pick up Penelope. Entities were now following her everywhere. She could see them clear as day, but she thought these were different. She was talking with one in particular; he was able to keep the bad ones away. His name was Ranar; he was the representative of a Council of 12. They needed human intervention with the evil that was loose at Clevis's property. Ranar informed her that we were the group that was going to put back what was released.

Henry lived in a doublewide in the Varsity Villa trailer park. The road to his place was very tidy, with tall pines everywhere and scenic streetlights. Henry's place was set back from the road. It was underneath the trees and away from the light. It wasn't foreboding; it was just very dark. Inside wasn't much brighter. Henry welcomed us in and we sat down. There was a light on in his kitchen plus one small dim lamp in the living room where we were. Penelope told Henry what had been going on. Dave and I gave an account of our visit. When we were done Henry walked out of the room, and then came back with a piece of pottery.

He handed it to me and asked, "So what do you think?"

It was black and dirty. When I say black, I mean blacker than a pit fire, like it had been under ground for centuries. It seemed to have a dark aura that made the air around it darker. The piece was heavy—heavier than it should been. In fact, I really didn't want to hold it for long. Just holding the piece made me feel uncomfortable, and even a little nauseous. "Here, take this back. I think it's not so bueno. Where did you find it?"

Henry laughed. "Don't worry about it. It's just a pre-Columbian chamber pot."

Dave later told me Henry had somehow retrieved it from a tomb in South America. Dave didn't think it was a chamber pot. He felt it was a funerary urn. It resembled the pots that sacrificed hearts were kept in.

Penelope started to tell Henry about the Council that had recently contacted her. All three of them tried to figure out exactly what and where this Council came from. Henry, however, in his all-knowing way, was convinced that the Council members were emissaries from the Pleiades star system. He had heard that lately they were taking a larger interest in terrestrial happenings.

Dave slightly rolled his eyes. "No. This is a spiritual group—Indian, I think."

Henry smirked. "Feather or dot?"

Dave's eyes narrowed. "What? Shut up! Dot, you dope! I think the demon may be Sumerian in origin. That would have it coming from the area of Persia. Close enough to the Indian subcontinent. Penelope feels the answer would be feather."

Henry pressed his newfound knowledge. "Isn't the Sumerian culture supposed to have originated in the Pleiaden or Aucturian star systems?"

Dave was impeccably ready. "The origin of the Sumerians is uncertain. It is generally believed that they probably migrated from the south through the Persian Gulf. However, their literature speaks of their homeland being Dilmun, which could have been of Indus Valley origin.

"But there is something else. Sumerians were also able to measure the distance between stars very precisely. They were incredible astronomers. The Sumerians assigned 12 'celestial bodies' to the solar system. These were the sun, the moon, and 10 planets. Until the late 18th century astronomers only knew of the six planets. Uranus was discovered in 1781, Neptune in 1846, and Pluto in 1930. The Sumerians 12th celestial body is yet to be discovered—a planet that they called Nibiru—and that is where they believed they came from. So while they believed they came from space, the Pleiades were never referred to by them as an origin."

Dave knew his stuff about the Sumerians. Henry knew what he read in whatever latest book he was engrossed in.

While they talked I was petting Henry's cat; she had come up to sit next to me on the couch. She was a nice tabby, purring up a storm. Her fur was light gray with very dark gray stripes. I noticed that as my focus would shift from the cat then back again, the patterns of her stripes were changing—not from me ruffling the fur, but major shifts. The cat looked me in the eye and smiled a little kitty smile when I started to notice the changes. This wasn't once or twice; it kept up for 15 minutes or more. The patterns on her fur would swirl. The size of the stripes would swell and shrink. When I couldn't take it anymore, I asked Henry what was going on. He and Dave just broke up. They told me she was Henry's familiar.

"She is just playing with your head. She loves to change the patterns on her fur whenever she meets someone new. She could tell you were seeing the shift. She just loves to have fun with it." Henry laughed.

Penelope just shook her head. She decided she needed a cigarette break. She walked out onto the little wooden front porch and closed the door. She came back a minute later looking rather shaken. Dave and Henry were deep in conversation, and didn't notice. Penelope called me over with a finger. She asked me to step outside with her.

It was dark outside, especially under the trees. Yet, the front yard was alive. Glowing green of all shapes and sizes flowed in and out of the yard, all around the trees. There had to be at least a dozen or more. It was a different green than we saw manifest at Clevis's property. This was more of a natural green. Just to the right of the porch was one blob that sat at the foot of a tree. It wasn't moving at all. I squinted hard. There was something there. I relaxed my eyes and let them just gaze at the spot. I thought it looked like a little man. He was in a siesta posture: arms around his knees, head bowed under a big floppy hat or sombrero. When he looked up at me it was evident that I was seeing more than my imagination. I was taken aback, startled but not frightened.

"Are you seeing what I'm seeing?" Penelope asked nonchalantly.

"Oh, yeah. I see them!"

She sighed in relief. We stood on the porch and watched the show. It was a ballet of light. Some of the shimmering shapes were scurrying around on the ground. Some glowing blobs were floating about in the air, just milling about, in and out of the trees. The songs of the crickets and the frogs were making a wonderful chorus. It was enchanting, albeit a little spooky. All the while the little guy at the base of the tree just looked up at me intently from under the brim of his hat. We went back in.

I grabbed Dave and said, "Hey, there's something you should really see outside."

When he and I walked out on to the porch, I figured it would all be gone. It was still there. Dave's van was parked on the street about 150 feet away. It was backlit by the bright pool of a distant streetlamp. The air out on the street was foggy and isolated. In this little bubble that seemed to be disconnected from reality, everything was crystal clear. It was our own creepy little fairyland.

Dave looked over at the little man, and said rather dryly, "He's here for you." There was a pause as he let the statement sink in. "That is your ally. He is here to help you with your upcoming endeavors. Or perhaps, teach you how to play the banjo. You need to relax yourself; let your eyes almost cross. Look at him. You have a genuine sombrero-wearing midget for an ally. You should be proud!"

I focused all my attention on the ally. I looked at the details of his clothing. I noticed how even sitting against the tree his bearing was relaxed yet powerful. He had a strong face and bushy moustache. You could call it weathered. I could feel a strong connection. I was comforted to know he was on my side.

Dave snickered, "It's interesting that your ally would look like the Frito Bandito."

Then it got quiet. Dead quiet. Our little bubble burst. The dancing shapes fled or just blinked out. Picture the coral reef as the shadow of a huge predator crosses over. Everything stopped! The little man's gaze deeply intensified.

It could be felt before you could see it, out on the road, floating at about head high. There it was: this big, green floating orb of dull light. And the disturbing part was it was moving directly toward us. This wasn't the good, nature green. It was about 4 feet (1.2 meters) across at the very least. It seethed with a malevolent intelligence. It exuded *bad*. The anger and hatred poured off of it in waves. As we stared at the ball the world stopped. The malicious sphere made no sound as it slowly floated over to Dave's van. There were no sounds at all—none. It wasn't cool and fun anymore; it was terrifying. The thing circled the van. Then, to my horror, whatever it was floated into one of the open windows. It lit up the interior, moving around, searching, looking, hating. The orb popped out of the other window and slowly floated down the street, continuing on its way. Everything seemed to hold its breath.

When the globe floated out of sight the night woke back up. The crickets and frogs started to sing. We were back to our reality again. The iniquity that had invaded our senses dissipated. The ally looked very intently at me. I could feel the acknowledgment from him; this was the enemy we were going to have to face. The door behind us opened. We turned around to see Penelope beckoning us in. I turned back around and saw the ally was gone.

Henry stared intently at us as we walked in, "What was that? I felt something at the perimeter of the property."

Dave smiled his wicked smile. "We must have been closing in on the truth. It was a ball of pure evil. I've never seen anything like it."

Henry was very put out. He said, "I've spent many years building up the defenses around my place. That's why it couldn't come into the yard. I did hear it knock! What was that? I really want to know now. I need to see this haunted property. We have to figure out a way to get over there."

Penelope agreed to find out when Clevis would be going out of town so we could visit the property as a group. This time Penelope would stay away. We felt that for her safety she should not go back. Of course, trespassing on somebody's property was the least of our worries, it would turn out. But those thoughts were alien phantoms to us as we planned and plotted our return to Clevis's world.

Chapter 7

Some Lessons Learned

Black Eagle

You must eliminate all the incredible clutter piled in your life. You are a hoarder. You need to simplify your world. Once you make a decision, banish your fears. Your decision should run them off and make you free like the wind. I tell you all the time that the most efficient way to live is as a warrior. Oh sure, it is fine to worry and seek counsel before you make any decision, but once you make it, soar like a hawk; there will be as many other decisions still awaiting you as there are points of light in the night sky. That's the warrior's way. When things become unclear, and you long for counsel, think of your death. The idea of death is the only thing that tempers our spirit. To be a warrior you have to be crystal clear. And you must be able to tolerate the smell of buffalo farts.

Robbie

My father gave me my first set of Tarot cards. Sometimes my dad would have to drive off base to pick up any forgotten items. I always begged for him to pick up a comic book. He wouldn't bring me *Richie Rich* or *Sad Sack*. He would come home with *Eerie*, *Creepy*, and *Vampirella*. I think those were the ones he secretly wanted to read.

Then he started to bring home *Man, Myth and Magic*. Now there was a magazine that treated the paranormal as real; it offered alternative realities that coexisted with ours. It opened my eyes. During this time I received the unusual gifts of the Ouija board and my first deck of Tarot cards.

I found that the cards talked to me. Not like "Hey, Robbie, what did you have for breakfast?" kind of talking, but I understood the relationships among the cards. I read the general descriptions; however, I could intuit something deeper. I worked intensely with the cards for a while. It dawned on me that I kept asking questions that I really didn't want to know the answer to. Or I would ask a painful question that I knew the answer to, in the grasping hope that the cards would come up with a more palatable response. Of course, that never happened. After a disturbing group experience with the Ouija board, I put the tools away. I didn't get rid of them; I just shelved them. Occasionally, when I was really perplexed, I would look to the cards for guidance. I found they just reiterated my intuition.

Dave felt I should start using the cards again. So I started throwing the Celtic Cross. This time there was something different. We were getting answers to questions, and I mean answers that we construed to be actual guidance. There might be something to this Council of Penny's. I could feel the outside help.

Dave also told me I should explore *The Teachings of Don Juan* a little deeper. He said that he thought my perception had shifted. I might gain some insight from another approach to what he was teaching me. I had tried to read the Castaneda books several times in the past. They never really did anything for me. The second half of the first book is horrid. I had to put grains of sand under my eyes to keep them open. This time was different. Now I could see how the lessons Don Juan tried to teach Carlos had a very real correlation with what was now happening to me. I started to understand his trials and experiences; they were becoming my trials and experiences. This is when the road trips began. Dave told me he had to make me accessible to power, whatever that meant.

We went to Lake Alice on the University of Florida campus. We were looking for places of power; at least that's what Dave said. He also said that places of power could be found in the weirdest places, from a park in the middle of a city to, in this case, a big lake full of alligators on a large college campus. We stopped where everyone went to see the resident bull gator, but there was no one there. It's a funny thing: When you are undertaking shamanistic acts there never seems to be anyone around. Dave likes to say that power needs no witnesses. Looking around the area, he seemed satisfied that there wasn't anyone there.

He told me, "I need to teach you how to find your power spot. In every place that you find yourself, there is a spot where you will feel the most comfortable. Is it your favorite chair, or is it the fact you feel most comfortable where the chair is sitting? Everyone has a power spot. I am going to teach you how to find yours."

He looked out over the lake, and then looked back at me. His eyes seemed unusually glassy. "If you relax your vision and just gaze out, no—no—don't try to look; just kind of gaze using your peripheral vision. Un-focus your eyes a little. What do you see? Take your time."

Suddenly, I did perceive something different, "I don't know. Maybe there's a dark spot over there. It's a circle; the grass isn't quite as bright."

"Okay. We can start with that. Go over and stand in this circle you see."

I walked over to stand where I thought the circle was. "What do I do now?"

"Hang there. We'll see."

The longer I stood there the worse I felt. This wasn't right. Then I started to get nauseous. I got more and more fidgety. I wasn't feeling well at all; I backed out of the circle.

Dave laughed. "Something wrong, Sherlock?"

Sometimes I think Dave enjoyed my discomfort too much. Yet he seemed to know I had made the wrong choice.

"What was that? Is your power spot supposed to make you sick?"

Now he really let out a cackle. "There are also spots that do just the opposite. That's what you found. Nice try. Remember what that looked like. If you have to defend yourself you don't want to be standing where you're weakest. Not the place to be standing when you're picking up chicks, either. Relax; try again."

I tried to relax—just stare off into space. To my right I saw a spot that shimmered. It was a heat wave shimmer that was there, but just. It looked silvery in a way. "I think I might see something."

"Well?"

"After the last one I'm not so sure I want to."

"You already found the bad spot." He had an evil smirk on his face.

I walked over and stepped into the circle. I relaxed; I felt really awake. I could feel how different this space was compared to the other. This was a spot where I could sit down and maybe hang out for a while.

Three golden dragonflies swooped down at me. They were a deep bronze-gold. I had never seen dragonflies that color before. We moved around the shores of the lake to look for other spots. As we walked, they continued to follow us. Occasionally one or two would land on my hat or outstretched hand.

Dave looked over as the dragonflies landed on me again. "If you have a really unusual encounter with a creature of nature it could be your totem. If you dream of the same animal of whatever species three times in a row, that could be your power animal. Or if you see three of the same animals acting in an abnormal way at the same time. You know like...." He waved his hand at the dragonflies. "They could be one of your totems."

We kept up the walk until dusk sent us to the van. The dragonflies followed us until we climbed in and drove away. But I was very curious; I wanted to know more. "Tell me about totems," I said.

Dave went into teaching mode. It really always took me off guard. It was like he became someone else for a bit. "Robbie, symbolic objects that have or form a connection with your totem spirit are used to get in touch with specific qualities found within an animal, which the person needs, connects with, or feels a deep affinity toward. Those objects are something that one keeps in their medicine bag. A medicine bag is where a shaman keeps the secrets to his power—his medicine. It is for you to carry various items that you will find, or that will be given to you, that have supernatural power. While anyone may have one, every medicine man *will* have one. As something that holds supernatural items, the medicine bag itself must have supernatural power of its own. You will be making a medicine bag and gathering items to fill it. Today we started that process.

"The first thing you need to place in the bag is four kernels of the corn I gave you, one for each direction of the wind. But you must let the corn select itself for those directions, and you must never forget which kernel is which. Medicine items endowed with various supernatural attributes will be gathered for the bag and they will come to you. You must pay attention. Do not miss a single gift that is presented to you in the coming days."

He paused for a minute, and looked almost sad. "I wish we had time for you to do a true vision quest. You will be doing several quests in the coming weeks. You will do these quests to stalk and gather power, to find yourself, and to become a warrior. These little ceremonies will not be the grand tribal affairs that are practiced by the Indians. We have no time for that now. Instead we will go to specific places to learn specific things. I don't care if you learn, or you think you have learned, because I am more concerned with teaching the lessons to your body. Your body will know, and eventually it will tell you. But I can tell you that to gain power, you must make personal sacrifices. Examples of this would be fasting and prayer. But in the end it is an elaborate system of the Earth. Our purpose is to make contact with natural spiritual forces that help and guide people to reach their potential. The spirits and totem guides will aid you in your quest to gather magical items, increase your knowledge, and aid your personal growth. Or you will simply die a horrible death in the attempt."

"I can't tell you how reassuring that is."

"I didn't promise you a rose garden! I promised you totem spirits. An animal guide is a power. The power of that animal is yours to have—for power—for guidance—for help. It gives it to you freely, and of its own accord. It is the animal's essence in you. You don't say, for example, 'I have the power of the dragonfly'; rather, you say, 'I *am* Dragonfly.' This is because if that is your animal, you will simply be Dragonfly.

"You can have several animal totems throughout your life. Sometimes an animal guide will come into your life for a short period of time, only to be replaced by another, depending on the journey or direction you are headed toward. Your guide will instruct and protect you as you learn how to navigate through your spiritual and physical life. When you find an animal that speaks strongly to you or you feel you must draw more deeply into your life, fill your environment with images of the animal to let it know it is welcome in your heart. Animal guides can help you get back to your Earthly roots, and reconnect with nature by reminding you that we are all interconnected. It can also help save your life. If you can figure out which animal is your totem, you will have gained a great deal of personal power. Just like that." He snapped his fingers.

"Today you got a tease. You had a display that was strictly for you. What you choose to do with the information is your decision. I can only take you to places and make you accessible to what you attract. So far your fate has touched the insect kingdom. I suspect you have other encounters in store for your efforts. Eventually you might want to select one and lure it to be your own. If it accepts you, it will be a good day to die. All will be right in your world. But it is the animal's choice. So when you chose which animal to court, choose well. Or you might be chosen by a creature whether you want it or not. It will be what you need as you walk your path." He smiled.

"My animal is Coyote. He is mine because my benefactor was also Coyote. Coyote found me, though I secretly wanted Coyote to pick me."

Chapter 8

More Lessons Learned

Black Eagle

You must become a warrior. Nothing else matters in the world. A warrior takes responsibility for all of his actions, no matter how grand, no matter how small. He exercises his patience, fully knowing that he is waiting, and knowing fully what he is waiting for. That is the warrior's way. Why do I have to tell you this so many times? You honestly have crow droppings for brains!

Robbie

We headed south out of Gainesville on 441 across Paynes Prairie. Dave said something about another lesson. I figured we were going to Micanopy, a small town on the other side of the grasslands. There were several reputed haunted houses there. When we got to the turnoff, instead of turning right, we turned left toward Rochelle.

It was a beautiful afternoon, almost cool in the shade. We headed east on County Road 234. We drove in the flitting shadows of the tall pines that lined the road. Every now and then we would get extended relief from the sun as we drove by hammocks of thick forest. The smell of the pines was profuse, occasionally cut by the deep wet perfume of the hidden lake or wetland we would pass. As we came around a bend we saw one of those little, green signs warning of a cemetery ahead. Dave started to slow down. There was a small parking area outside of a very old black fence. The wrought-iron gate gave us the name: Oak Ridge Cemetery.

A Florida state historical marker outside the gate explains the centerpiece of the cemetery. You could tell which one it was—a large white granite monument meant to be noticed. When you enter the first thing that strikes you is the age of the place. The governor's tomb is in the sunlight, but then the land slopes down and away from the road with its friendly sunshine. The woods on each side of the cemetery are impenetrable, being the edge of the Lochloosa game preserve. The back fence was lost in the looming darkness of the eldritch forest's shadows. The thick oak canopy and Spanish moss soaked up most of the light that was struggling to remain. There are not a lot of oaks in the graveyard itself, but the ones that are there are ancient. They have had many years to soak up the "fertilizer" and grow heavy with foliage.

I walked over to the governor's tomb and slowly walked around it. I tried to feel the energy. This was, after all, the most significant tomb here. It even had a historical marker.

Dave shook his head. "What are you doing?"

"Well, look at these digs. We're here to see the governor, right?"

He rolled his eyes and gave me that sardonic glare. "As someone once said to me, 'Can you become a bigger dope than you already are?' Come on. Follow me and quit fooling around."

As we headed down into the adumbral cemetery the canopy got thicker. The light penetrated even less. The gravesites were neat though—very well maintained. Some family plots even had little fences marking them off. There was very little underbrush; the trees had been able to keep the sun off this place for quite a while. Pine was no longer the dominant scent. Here under the green was the smell of autumn leaves morphing into rich soil.

Dave continued to lead me further back and deeper into the gloom. The markers at that end were covered with moss. The inscriptions were much harder to make out. There were less of them down there, too. I also noticed that there were a few depressions in the ground with no headstone. Poor pioneers that could only afford a wooden marker or no marker at all. Or maybe someone stole their marker. I shuddered at that thought.

Dave was heading toward the huge oak that dominated the bottom back of the graveyard. Finally he stopped. I noticed that we had reached a spot where there were four small, homemade markers, covered with green mold and fungi. He gestured down at one of the markers that had a pointed top to it. It was set off a little from the other three. It looked very odd. It was small, like for a child.

Dave grinned wolfishly and pointed directly at it. "So check this one out."

I leaned in to take a closer look. Unlike all of the other headstones, this one was made from poured concrete—not marble or stone, just poured concrete. Someone cast it in their backyard. In it was scratched the epitaph "Not Dead." There was nothing else on the stone. No name, no nothing—just "Not Dead." It was certainly homemade judging from the crudeness of the inscription; it was scratched in with a stick no less. The whole aura of the place was oppressive.

Dave leaned over to me and whispered, "Touch it."

"What?"

"It's just a gravestone. Touch it."

Once again common sense and reasoning ran screaming into the shadows. Like a dope I reached out.

POP!

"Owww!"

Working around lighting systems for shows, I know a shock when I get one. I pulled my hand quickly up and away. I drew an arc, 2 to 3 feet of blue crackling energy. It felt just like getting tagged with electric current. The after-image was momentarily burned on my retinas.

I turned to Dave in horror and amazement. "What was that?"

He was lying on the ground. I thought he was hurt.

"What's wrong with you?" I looked closer.

My friend Dave was shaking, holding his stomach, tears rolling down his face—laughing!

"It's not that funny!"

"You should have seen the look on your face, amigo!"

By the time we had returned home, it really was that funny. Once we were well away and blasting down the country roads, I could see the humor. I was still a little sore with it being at my expense. We came in laughing hard. Leigh and our roommate, Crystal, were sitting in the living room.

When we finished laughing after retelling the tale and I had finished cussing Dave out again, Crystal said she wanted to see.

"I won't go back out there today," I immediately blurted out, and everybody laughed.

Crystal was the perfect roommate at the time. Though she wanted to see the "Not Dead" grave, she didn't believe it shocked me. She didn't believe in ghosts, either. In fact she slept in one of the most active rooms in our house but it never bothered her. I don't think she realized what that cold spot was that was outside her door. Some people are just blessed....

The house was highly active. My first indication was the flashing light in Leigh's studio. It scared me. Not because of a haunting, but I thought there was an electrical short. I looked everywhere that didn't take knocking a hole in the wall. The wiring was fine. Quite by accident, Leigh discovered that if you said good morning to that room, the flashing stopped and the light worked fine.

There was a confirmation for me that the haunting was intelligent. I was digging around in the over-filled attic, in my bare feet. I heard the phone ring. I was a freelancer, so that phone was my source of income; I could not miss a call. I tiptoed as fast as I could through the attic and then bolted down the narrow staircase. I rushed down too fast. I had made sure the door was secured so the kitties couldn't join me upstairs. I was coming down a lot faster than I had intended. I rolled my shoulder, and I prepared for the imminent collision.

The doorknob turned and the door swung open. I know the cats hadn't all of a sudden grown opposable thumbs. I yelled my thanks and grabbed the phone. At that moment, I knew it wasn't a residual haunting.

Things didn't manifest every day but it was a fairly regular occurrence. Crystal was able to explain off everything. That can be an asset in a haunted house. It didn't mean she was unwilling to check out the graveyard. It was a few days before we made it back.

We headed down to the far end following Dave. Everyone else followed; I sort of meandered. I wasn't ready to go too close to the "Not Dead" stone. Dave stopped and pointed to the little, dark, moss-covered stone.

"Not Dead." He smiled at Crystal.

"Ouch. That's spooky. I guess you guys weren't lying. What would happen if I touched it?"

Dave shrugged his shoulders. "Why don't you see?"

I waited for the yelp and flash. Crystal touched the stone. Nothing.

"Robbie, why don't you show the girls what happened?" Dave was snickering.

"Oh, I don't think that's necessary."

"Come on. It'll be interesting." Dave was laughing hard now. "Aren't you kind of being a wimp?"

"Doesn't matter. I'll be standing over here."

David

"Robbie, can you be ready in half an hour?"

"Sure. For what?"

"Road trip—Paynes Prairie. You have a date with power."

As I hung up the phone I gathered my medicine bag and pipe. I thought about all the things Robbie still needed to learn. One of them was to manipulate the elements. On the prairie, there was a great chance that the wind would present itself. If I could get him to open up, he just might let the wind in to do its thing. If not, it was going to be a long autumn. I loaded my stuff into the van, fired up the engine, and spun out of the driveway, heading across town to Robbie's house.

"Should I bring anything with me?"

"Did you get a medicine bag?"

"Yeah, but there's not a lot in it yet."

"Bring it and anything else you feel you should."

I headed back out to the van and sat down inside to wait. I was curious to see what Robbie brought with him. This was another test. I had told him he was going to have a date with power. What he brought with him would reveal what he had learned so far.

Robbie surprised me. When he came out he had a powerful crystal hanging from his ear and a necklace with a Toltec totem, and was carrying his medicine bag. I just smiled.

"What are you grinning at now?"

"You. You are ready to dance with the wind."

I opened up the van as we made our way out on the prairie, hitting more than 100 miles per hour across U.S. 441. We shot like an arrow between Gainesville and Micanopy; the sun was partially hidden by the gathering clouds as it slowly sank in the western sky. It was early evening, already getting dark. We pulled into the lot on the south side of the prairie and parked near the trail entrance. We walked for about 20 minutes until we were in the middle of the vast savannah. All the way out I was talking to Robbie about power and the wind. It was lesson time:

"One of the vital elements of becoming a medicine man, as I have told you over and over, is to gather personal power. One of the ways to do that is to open yourself up to the elements and drink them in. Once you do, you will be able to persuade them into helping you. The elements are powerful allies to have. Today, I want you to play with the wind. I want you to get it to blow from all four cardinal directions. Right now, the wind is out of the west. When we leave, I want it to also be out of the west. But in between, I want you to move it around."

"How am I supposed to do that?"

"By exercising your will—and by being impeccable, of course."

I started laughing after I watched his expression change.

Robbie asked me something he had never asked me before: "Why are you always laughing? You laugh when you are talking to me seriously, or when something really weird happens, and freaks me out. Sometimes I can see the humor and I know sometimes you gotta laugh 'cause there's nothing else."

"I laugh a great deal because I like to laugh, yet everything I say is deadly serious. Don't let my amusement confuse you into thinking it's all a joke. I assure you, it is not. You could die out there today. It's getting dark now. The world is different at this time of the day. We are very visible here; something is coming to us. Look over there!"

I pointed to an area that was high grass. It was twirling and twisting as if something were moving through it.

"That's just the wind, Dave. Isn't it just the wind?"

"It may seem like the wind to you, because the wind is all you know. Look! Here it comes. Notice how it seems to be searching for us. I guarantee you it is not the wind. It's something that hides in the wind. It looks like a whorl, something twisting around in spite of the direction the wind is blowing. But if you watch the high grass closely, you will notice that it is only in a small area that the twirling takes place. Yet there is nothing there to make the wind do this in so small an area. It is moving in a specific direction. It either tumbles or it twirls. A hunter must know all that in order to move correctly."

"It's just the wind, Dave. All I see is grass blowing."

"Don't be a dope, Robbie. To believe that the world is only as you think it is, is foolish. The world is a mysterious place. It is especially weird in the twilight. It is called the crack between the worlds for a reason. Things can seep out, things can seep in. That thing is seeping in, and it is heading for you. This is what you need to understand. That thing can follow us. It can make us tired. It might even kill us. At this time of the day, in the twilight, there is no wind. At this time there is only power."

"You know, I think I understand. When the sun goes down, the wind changes. It blows from one direction during the day, but then it stops. After dark, it starts again, often from a different direction."

"That's right, Robbie. If you lived out here in the wilderness you would know that during the twilight the wind is power. A hunter that knows his stuff is keenly aware of this; he acts based on his knowledge. He uses the twilight and that power. Now, here is the caveat: If it is convenient to him, the hunter can hide from the power by covering himself and remaining motionless until the twilight is gone, then the power has sealed him into its protection."

"What are you babbling about?"

"The protection of the power seals you like a fortress. A hunter can stay out in the open and no panther, coyote, or rattlesnake can bother him. A buffalo could come up to the hunter's nose and sniff him; if the hunter does not move, the buffalo would simply leave. I can guarantee you that."

"I don't think I want to try that!"

"Are you sure? There are buffalo out here. No? Okay. You don't have to tonight. Tonight we have something different to learn. If the hunter *wants* to be noticed all he has to do is to stand boldly out in the open at the time of the twilight. Power will pester him and seek him all night. So, if a hunter wants to travel at night or if he wants to be kept awake he must make himself available to the wind. So here is tonight's lesson and the secret of great hunters; you must learn to be available or unavailable at the exact moment it is required. You must learn to become deliberately available and unavailable. The way you live now, you are available all the time. To be unavailable does not mean to hide or to be secretive, but instead to be inaccessible. It makes no difference to hide if everyone knows that you are hiding."

"That just seems like fool talk."

"Look, man. We are all fools. You, my friend, are no different. At one time in my life I made myself available over and over again until there was nothing of me left for anything except perhaps whining. That is exactly what I did. I whined constantly about not having enough time, or not having this thing or that thing. It was stupid. But you have to do what I did. You have to escape! You must get out of the middle of the road. Your entire being is there, standing out in the open. If you shot off a flare gun you would be no more visible than you are right now. If you try to hide now, you would only imagine that you are hidden. Being in the middle of the road means that everyone passing by watches your comings and goings. This includes the power that is now racing toward you from out there!" I pointed to the turbulence approaching Robbie at a very fast pace.

"Holy cow!"

I placed my hand on his shoulder. "Steady, little buddy. The art of a hunter is to become inaccessible, and to be inaccessible means that you touch the world around you sparingly. You don't expose yourself to the power of the wind unless it is mandatory. Except tonight, it is mandatory! You cannot escape it now, it is far too late. Now accept your date with the wind."

Robbie

"What exactly did I do? If I have no idea, how can I do it again?"

Dave just grinned. He shrugged his shoulders. "You had your date with the wind. You made it change directions several times. At one point, it was spinning you around; you may have been a foot or two off the ground. It was too much for your rational mind to deal with! But your body learned the lesson, and that's what matters, so while you don't know, your body does. In time your body will teach it to your mind. In the meantime, trust your body. It may save your life. But there is another lesson here.

"You don't use or drain people until they have shriveled up to nothing, especially the people you love. By knowing when to be unavailable, you deliberately avoid exhausting not only yourself but also the other people around you. You are not hungry and desperate because a hunter knows he will lure game into his clutches time and time again, so he doesn't worry. If you worry, you become accessible, albeit unwittingly accessible. Because once you worry, you cling out of desperation; once you cling, you are going to get exhausted and exhaust whoever or whatever you are clinging to."

The first heavy drops of rain began to fall as we reached the van.

Chapter 9

The Devil's Millhopper

Black Eagle

The will is something that is very special. No one can explain how it happens, or how it works as it happens very mysteriously. There is no way of knowing how to use it, how to predict its arrival, or where it even comes from. What is known is that the results of using it are incredible. You must start by knowing you can develop your will. A warrior knows this and proceeds to wait for it. A warrior knows that he is waiting and he knows what he is waiting for. You are such a dope! I can't believe I am still telling you this!

The average person almost never knows what they are waiting for. In fact, the average person is waiting for his favorite TV show, or some other mindless buffalo dung. A warrior, however, has no problems; he knows that he is waiting for his will. Will is something very clear and powerful which can direct your acts. Will is a tool a man uses to win a battle, which he, by all calculations, should lose. Right now beetle has more will than you have—and that is sad.

Robbie

The Devil's Millhopper earned its name from the prodigious amounts of animal bones and fossils found at the bottom by early settlers. It's a beautiful, peaceful little park. We pulled through the gates, looked, and breathed a sigh of enjoyment at the deserted parking lot. Even midweek there are usually a few people about. But whenever we are doing metaphysical stuff, it's like the world abandons us—or the other way around.

We got out of the van and started down the path. Each step along the sandy trek raised a puff of warm dust. The smell of the dry pine scrub filled our senses. Thick palmetto patches were all around. The pines slowly gave way to hardwood. The palmettos lost out to small trees and shrubs as we moved closer to the edge of the sink. Dave spoke as if he was reading my mind. It never ceased to surprise me. "You are always amazed that there is no one around, aren't you?"

"How—how did you know that?"

"Because, little brother, we are no longer in the world. We are between the worlds when we seek power. Power dwells between the worlds. It is our job to tap it, and take it as our own."

We continued on in silence. I reveled in the sight before me, seeing it like I had never seen it before.

It's a big hole, 500 feet (152.4 meters) across and 120 feet (36.5 m) deep, verdant green. A trail skirts the edge. Looking over, you could see the dense trees on the other side. When we got up to it, we could see the tops of trees on our side that were growing out of the hole. The staircase drops off the edge and heads down into a green abyss.

"This is an exercise in gathering power. You did bring that sage wand, didn't you?"

I showed it to him.

"Good. That will be an offering of scents and vibration to the spirits that are present. Sage has a very high resonance. It will attract beneficial spirits to you. It's also very protective, so it will repel anything nasty that might be around. Remember: We are no longer in our world. When we left the van, we entered the world of power. But there are other things besides power. Nasty things. Boogie men. When we get to the bottom of the sink, you must do a little prayer, then burn your sage. Relax into the energy. Just sit there and be. Soak it up."

We started down the stairs, which were comprised of steep switchbacks down the side of the one wall. The walkway crisscrossed one of the 12 springs that feed into the lush bottom. The ecosystem changed noticeably as we went deeper into the hole. The tall trees gave way to shorter trees and ferns. Farther down on the steeper sections of the walls the mosses, liverworts, and ferns cover and fill every nook and crevasse. The light down there was green—a different green than places I had recently encountered. The green was fed by the sunlight but coming from every tree and plant in the Millhopper. The deeper we descended, the cooler it got. The green embraced me; I felt at home, very relaxed. Around step 116 there is a small platform with a bench.

Dave suddenly stopped and said, "I think I'll stop here. You need to do this by yourself."

"What am I supposed to do?"

"Sit and be still. You'll know when you're done." With that he plopped down, kicked back, and then shooed me on.

As I climbed farther down, the walls slowly closed in. It was a relief to reach the coolness of the bottom. I sat on the bench slowly taking in the wonderland around me. It was GREEN—a good green, welcoming me, enfolding me. I was in a tropical rainforest. There were vines hanging everywhere: tall ferns, little dogwoods, magnolias, and rhododendron; it was a heavenly garden. The air was crisp—clean. I filled my lungs with the effervescent sparkle. The springs fed into little waterfalls ionizing the atmosphere. The clean clear water ran across the floor of the sink and then disappeared into the depths. Some of the runs just disappeared off into the green, while some of them flowed into the small caves that littered the area.

I took several breaths and started to just listen to the voices of the water. I could hear the slight rustle of the foliage as the birds flitted about. I felt comforted, held in the earth's arms. The sunlight coming down through the canopy created a sparkle effect everywhere. I lit the sage and began to give thanks for the beauty surrounding me. I apologized for any disturbance I might be causing. The smell of the smoke was uplifting.

As I put down the sage, I felt something land on my hand. It was one of the scourges of Florida. I knew it when I saw that flash of dirty yellow— a deerfly. They are tenacious little tormentors. You have to swat to kill, because if you just stun them they will come back hungrier. This one, however, just sat there on my hand. I looked a little closer. It had the most incredible deep golden, multifaceted eyes. As my hand moved its eyes sparkled and glittered like two jewels. It didn't bite me.

I turned and looked out. I was able to slowly relax my eyes and open my field of vision. I just gazed. The differences between light and shadow crystallized. The scene in front of me turned into a black and white negative as the color faded. The dichotomy of the black and white slowly melded into a field of glowing white. It was Home. It was Love. I sat for a while in the knowledge that I was not observing nature; I was a part of nature, connected, the same. We were one.

Gradually everything returned to almost normal. The plants and trees were glowing with color and energy—a fairy wonderland come to life. Everything in the foreground was in sharp relief, but it wasn't so on the far wall. The green on the other side was still a bit blurry. It was only 200 or so feet (61 m) away, but it swirled and coalesced in front of me. There was a being there. I could see the big round face with its quizzical expression. The outline of his body was plain as day. He was there on the wall. He was at least 20 feet (6 m) tall, but he was hunched down. That's good; I don't think I could have taken him looming over me. We made eye contact and sat in a meditation for I don't know how long. I was lost in the moment.

I thought about the sage. I lit it up to give a prayer of thanks to the spirits of the place and to the giant guardian that lived there. The whole time the deerfly just rode my hand. He was moving to be upright but didn't fly off and, a definite miracle, he still wasn't biting.

Then there was a shift. Time hiccupped—boom—back to the beautiful reality of Florida. The fairyland had retreated behind the shades of green. Reality was looking pretty good, though. Everything glowed. I could see the auras of all the living things, the ferns, the trees above me, and the damselflies flitting in and out of the stray sunrays that were making their way down. Even the flies had a small glow around them. I was relaxed and at peace. Finally, I knew it was time to go.

I said thank you again and started to climb. My new friend, the deerfly, joined me on the ascent. We started back up into the deep flora and falling waters. Up we climbed. When we reached Dave he looked at us, cocked an eyebrow, turned, and silently started to ascend. My little buddy and I followed behind him.

The climb up should have at least been a little strenuous, but for me it wasn't. I felt buoyant—totally alive, connected to all the life around me. The energy of the sink was lifting me up. When we had reached the top I thanked the deerfly for accompanying me on my walk. It looked up at me then buzzed off.

We stepped away from wooden stairway and started down the path. Around the first corner we heard a chorus of laughter and carryings-on. It slapped us back to reality. The everyday had returned; the magic went back to being hidden. I was back in the world.

"Robbie, you need even more personal power. Our quest for your personal power will involve going to many different locations where power lurks. Today we went to the Devil's Millhopper not because it is a unique and beautiful place, which it is, but because it reeks of power. Next, I need to show you how to find the 'Crack between the Worlds.' It's one of the old shaman rituals for gaining power. It is a point in time when it is neither daylight, nor dark; no rules apply, as the rules of day are cast to the wind, and the rules of the night have yet to take command. It is what I call the 'tween' time. What is important is that when you can find the crack between the worlds you can stop the world. At that specific moment when the world collapses, tremendous power can be acquired.

"There's no plan when it comes to hunting power. Hunting power or hunting game is really all the same. A hunter must always be in a state of readiness, because he never knows what to expect. Recently, when we sojourned out to the prairie, you learned about the hidden nature of the wind, and how the power it carries can be used as your own. As a result of that lesson, you are now quite capable of hunting power in the wind all by yourself. But there are other things you don't know about, which are, like the wind, the center of power at certain times and at certain places. Learning to recognize this, reading the signs will assist you in making yourself 'accessible' to power."

He looked at me to see if I was getting it. I put forward my very best look of understanding. He shrugged his shoulders and chuckled.

"As you are starting to realize, power is a very peculiar affair. It is impossible to pin it down and say what it really is. It is energy, but to you it will manifest as a feeling that you have about certain things or situations. It is a notion that you feel, but can't quite put your finger upon.

Power is also personal. It belongs to you alone. A hunter of power entraps it, then stores it away as his personal quarry, like charging some biological battery inside of you. Thus, as your personal power grows, you may acquire so much that you become what I call a man of knowledge."

We sat in silence for a moment listening to the crickets chirping.

Dave continued, "If you store this power, your body can perform unbelievable feats. On the other hand, if you dissipate all your power you'll be a fat old man who farts a lot in no time at all. A hunter of power watches everything and everything tells him some secret. How can one be sure that things are telling secrets? Simple: You just ask. The only way to be sure is by following all the instructions I have been giving you, starting from the first day you came to see me about this whole darn demon affair. In order to have power one must live with power. One must be accessible to it. I can't stipulate this enough."

The sudden silence around us in the yard was deafening. There was no traffic on the road in front of my house, which was odd at that time of the evening. Dave seemed not to notice. Maybe he had taken me out of the world again. Darn, I wish I could do that.

"There are worlds upon worlds, Robbie, right here in front of us. We only see one world with our eyes, but let me assure you, we can only see the tip of the iceberg. These unseen worlds are nothing to laugh at. Your death lurks in one of them. The ally lurks in another. Still others contain those who have lived before us. One even has demons. To handle all the layers of reality requires tremendous personal power. The comical thing is that power commands you and yet it is at your command."

Dave stopped for a second, listening to the silence. He lowered his voice like he didn't want to be heard by some unseen entity. "I told you already that power is a very weird affair. In order to have it and command it one must have power to begin with. It is like a catch-22 of sorts; consequently, I have to give you power so you can seek power. It is possible, however, to store it, little by little, until one has enough to sustain oneself in a battle of power.

"But to start, one must have a benefactor to bestow some essence on to you. This is what I have been doing with you since this began. You are weak in the realm of power. You are also like a wide open door.

I told you once you started down this path there was no turning back. Now you have to learn or you will perish! To hedge my bet, I have to give you power. To do that, I have to take you to where power dwells and summon it to you. What you do with it, of course, is your affair alone. All I can do is stack the deck in your favor. The rest is up to you."

As quickly as the silence came, it left. Traffic began to pass my house and the crickets began their concert, much louder it seemed than before.

"The world is a mystery. This—what you're looking at—is not all there is to it. We are just a gnat in a multiverse of realities. There is much more to the world—so much more, in fact, it is endless. So when you're trying to figure it out, all you're really doing is trying to make the world familiar. You and I are right here, in the world that you call real, simply because we both know it. You don't know the world of power; therefore you cannot make it into a familiar scene. But soon—very soon—you will, and you will realize that there are no words for it. You can't speak of it, you can only experience it.

"You have to go to the crack between the worlds and make yourself accessible to power."

"Okay. Where can I find this crack between the worlds?"

"That's easy. Gwen's place."

I didn't like the grin Dave had as he replied.

Chapter 10

Gwen's Place

Black Eagle

A detached man, who knows he has no possibility of avoiding his death, has only one thing to defend himself with: the power of his decisions. He has to be the master of his choices. He must fully understand that his choice is his responsibility and, once he makes it, there is no longer time for whining or regrets. His decisions are final, simply because death does not permit him time to cling to anything. I cannot emphasize this enough! But don't take my word for it; ask your death. He is sitting right over there!

Robbie

We headed southeast out of Gainesville. The smells of late summer filled the air. The ride out was spotted with the occasional small homestead or farm breaking up the continuous stands of pine trees. Dave was talking at me, as usual: "You know, stopping the world is an appropriate appellation of certain states of awareness, in which the reality of everyday life is altered because the flow of our interpretation, which ordinarily runs endlessly, uninterruptedly, has been stopped by a set of circumstances alien to that flow. In this case, the set of circumstances alien to our normal flow of interpretations is the shamanic description of the world. The precondition for stopping the world is that one has to be convinced; in other words, one has to learn the new description in a total sense for the purpose of pitting it against the old one. That way you break the dogmatic certainty, which we all share, that the validity of our perceptions or our reality is not to be questioned."

"You mean seeing everything, like the forest, and ignoring the trees?"

"No. More like seeing everything, and realizing the trees are elephant farts. Our reality is a projection that we hold as true because we have been programmed that this is so. To us it is very real, but it is just a projection, like a hologram, on the world of power. It keeps rational men sane. But then we are not rational men. We are warriors."

We took some turns, then headed down a long, dirt road. The pine hammock gave way to old oaks, laurels, and Spanish moss.

"How is your dreaming coming along?"

Dave had talked to me for some time about dreaming—about learning to control my dreams. He said it was the secret to the double. Something I didn't quite grasp. But he maintained that if you could look at your hands in your dreams, you could seize control of your dream and do whatever you wished.

"I've tried but I haven't seen my hands yet," I replied. "What does that have to do with the double? Why do I need to develop one?"

"No one develops a double, Robbie. That's only a way of talking about it. All of us luminous beings, *and we ARE all luminous beings*, have a double. All of us! Each and every person in the world, no matter whether they are a genius or a dope, has a double. The old hag that works at the Suwannee Swifty who scares all the children to death with her toothless grin? She has a double. You—*you* have a double.

"The difference is a warrior learns to be aware of it, that's all. There are seemingly insurmountable barriers protecting that awareness. But that's to be expected; the barriers are what make arriving at that awareness such a unique challenge.

"You are afraid of it because you're thinking that the double is what the word says—a doppelganger—or, in other words, another you. I chose the word in order to describe it. The double is oneself. It cannot be faced in any other way. Some might say it is the essence of our self, but it is more than that. In a way it is a manifestation of our spirit.

"The double is not a matter of personal choice. Neither is it a matter of personal choice as to who is selected to learn the shamanic knowledge that leads to that awareness. Have you ever asked yourself, why you in particular? I don't mean that you should ask it as a question that begs an answer, but in the sense of a warrior's pondering on his great fortune, the fortune of having found a challenge."

Dave chuckled. "To make it into an ordinary question is the device of a conceited ordinary man who wants to be either admired or pitied for it. I have no interest in that kind of question, because there is no way to answer it. The decision of picking you was a design of power; no one can discern the designs of power, not me, not you, not Einstein. Now that you've been selected, there is nothing that you can do to stop the fulfillment of that design. Except give up the ghost and die maybe. But that would be cheating."

"Wait a minute. So I have no choice?"

"A warrior is in the hands of power. His only freedom is to choose an impeccable life. *That* is your choice." He chuckled again.

"You're in a terrible spot. It's too late for you to retreat but too soon to act. All you can do is witness. For you there is only witnessing acts of power and listening to stories, the tales of power, the stories of high medicine. The double is just one of those vignettes. You know that, and that's why your reason is so taken by it. You are beating your head against a wall if you pretend to understand. All that I can say about it, by way of explanation, is that the double, although it is arrived at through dreaming, is as real as it can be. It is the self. It is the awareness of our state as luminous beings. It can do anything, yet it chooses to be unobtrusive and gentle."

We turned at a gate and headed down the drive. Gwen's house was hidden in the thick shrubbery. It was very hard to discern from the landscape. The Spanish moss that hung from all the trees was mirrored in the spiderwebs that hung everywhere around the eaves. The windows on the sides of the house were very small slits peering out of the greenery. Swamp Witch Gwen...

Her place had been officer's quarters at Camp Blanding and had been used during World War II. They sold it off as surplus in the '50s. Someone thought it would make a nice lake cottage.

The entrance foyer and kitchen had low ceilings that felt cramped. It was deceiving. The farther back into the house you went the more open it became. When you stepped out on to the back porch the spacing between the trees opened up. It was a very nice bit of heaven.

Down at the bottom of the slope of the backyard was a canal. Looking out through the oaks and cypress, there was the hint of reflected light. It looked as if it could be from a small lake. There was no telling what the canal could lead to. In that part of Florida it could be a lake, a river, or even another canal.

Dave and Gwen's dog pack took me down to the canal. He said it led to a midsized lake. The channel wasn't well kept. The trees formed a tunnel out to the big water; a couple of canoes littered the shore. There was a path cut through the water hyacinths, indicating the boats went out often. The area off to the right was very swampy. Tall cattails and cane grass sprung up everywhere, taller than my head, obscuring a good look at the lake.

We walked along the edge of this area until we came to a trail that headed into the tall brush of the swamp. Whereas we had stayed on the edge of the marsh, the dogs would wade into the ankle deep water. But now they stuck to the path. When you could look down through the brush, the water was getting deeper and darker. We left the canopy of the trees but still had the lake hidden by all the tall reeds. We rounded a corner to find that the path widened out to a small landing on a beautiful lake. About half a mile to the west, the cypresses of the opposing shoreline were tall against the sky. It looked like a postcard promoting old Florida. It was a little spot of paradise.

I became aware of a floating sensation. I realized we were at the edge of the plant growth. That meant some fairly deep water surrounded us, but we were on a path we had followed out. How could we be floating? I was confused.

Dave noticed the perplexed look on my face. He said, "I told you Gwen was a powerful swamp witch. This is one of her altars. The plants have grown and woven the path out here that supports us above the water. We are indeed floating on an organic island, hovering over the deep."

If you just relaxed and stood there you couldn't tell it wasn't solid ground. But I noticed if you bounced up and down it felt like we were on a floating dock. We were on a suspended walkway made of living plants.

"When I leave, I want you to stand out here on the edge of the peninsula. Gaze out at the other side of the lake. When the sunset is coming to an end, as the last vestiges of the sun blink below the horizon, there will be a spark—a flash of light. That, my friend, is the crack between the worlds. When you see that you will be able to stop the world."

"Yeah, well. How do I do that?"

Dave smiled and walked away, leaving me answerless at the lake. No matter how many times I practiced this over the next few weeks, the result was mostly the same: The sun would take forever to set. When I went in it was pitch black and hours later. I have no idea where the time went. Dave would laugh hysterically.

"I swear I just saw the spark. What time is it? I swear the sun just now finished setting."

"It's 10:30. There are times your rational mind can't deal with the lessons you are learning. It veils the experience until you are energetically able to deal with it."

"Darn, I'm hungry. It always takes the sun so long to set."

Dave reached into a leather pouch, and then he handed me some jerky. "Here eat some of this. It's venison—power food. It will help ground you."

A couple of bites and my hunger faded. But the world never stopped. At least, I don't think it did?

Chapter 11

Return to Clevis's

Black Eagle

I will tell you this: A warrior treats absolutely everything with respect and does not trample on anything unless he has to. He does not abandon himself to anything, not even to his death. He is never a willing partner, he is not available, and if he involves himself with something, you can be sure that he is aware of what he is doing. For a warrior there is nothing out of control. Life for a warrior is an exercise in strategy. You joke around and say you want to find the meaning of life. A warrior doesn't give a hoot about meanings. He lives his life strategically. Therefore, if he couldn't avoid an accident he would find means to equalize the effects, sidestep the consequences, or battle against them. He fights to the very end. I can't tell you this enough: A warrior is never available; never is he standing on the road waiting to be clobbered. On the contrary, if trouble lies in his path, he simply changes directions. Thus he cuts to a minimum his chances of the unforeseen. Just remember that a warrior is never idle and never in a hurry.

Robbie

Dave was spewing out the koans. "You say you've heard that some masters of Eastern esoteric doctrines demand absolute secrecy about their teachings. Perhaps those masters are just indulging in being masters. I'm not a master; I'm only a warrior. So I really don't know what a master feels like. But I know this: It doesn't matter what one reveals or what one keeps to oneself. Everything we do—everything we are—rests on our personal power—period. If we have enough of it, one word uttered to us might be sufficient to change the course of our lives. However, if we don't have enough personal power, the most magnificent piece of wisdom in all of creation can be revealed to us and that revelation won't make a bit of difference."

"Isn't wisdom universal? If you hear great wisdom, no matter what it is, you should be able to act upon it."

"Not so, and I'll prove it to you right now. I'm going to utter perhaps the greatest piece of knowledge anyone can voice. Let me see what you can do with it." Dave became animated, using theatrics and wild gestures. It was going to be a long night. "Do you know that at this very moment you are surrounded by eternity? And do you know that you can use that eternity, if you so desire?"

He leaped up onto the coffee table. "There! Eternity is there! All around! Do you know that you can extend yourself forever in any of the directions I have pointed to? Do you know that one moment can be eternity? This is not a riddle; it's a fact, but only if you mount that moment and use it to take the totality of yourself forever in any direction."

It looked like rationality had finally taken a permanent vacation. He continued, "You didn't have this knowledge before; now you do. I have revealed it to you, but it doesn't make a bit of difference, because you don't have enough personal power to utilize my revelation. Yet if you did have enough power, my words alone would serve as the means for you to round up the totality of yourself and to get the crucial part of it out of the boundaries in which it is contained."

He tapped my chest and said, "Your body is the boundary I'm talking about. You can get out of it. We are a feeling—an awareness encased here. We are luminous beings, for a luminous being only personal power matters."

Dave answered the phone on the first ring. Darn, it was like he was waiting for the call.

Several days later, while my head was still reeling from the grand revelation, I received some opportune news. "Hey, Dave. Penny just called. Clevis called and asked if she could come by and feed his dog for a couple of days. He's going out of town. This might be our only chance to get Henry and Gwen over there."

"Swell! I'll call Gwen and then let Henry know. What did Penelope say about feeding the dog?"

"She thought about it and discussed it with her new entourage. It was decided it wouldn't be prudent. We should be clear if we get there about 9 p.m. Penelope is still officially a tenant, so we do have a valid reason to be there."

"I guess the Council thinks it's okay for us to go, then," Dave snickered. Even I smiled a little at that one.

With impeccable timing, Dave and I pulled up just as Gwen parked on the street in front of Penelope's house. As Dave killed the engine, Henry showed up behind us. We walked collectively to the driveway. As the group crossed the culvert and stepped onto the property there was a collective gasp from Gwen and Henry.

"Wow—that's different." Henry seemed taken aback.

"Yeah, ain't it a kick?"

"*Kick* is the right word."

Gwen piped up, interrupting Henry and me: "Give us the nickel tour, Dave."

"Greetings. I'm Dave Rountree, your tour guide from Hell. We can start over here at Penelope's, where this week's feature haunt is a glowing demon of darkness...."

I had already had the pleasure of a tour, so I wandered around on my own to see what impression I could get after dark without Clevis around. I slowly edged my way to the big oak at the side of the bungalow. I wanted to stand under the branch that been the catalyst of my visions of the whipping when we had last trekked around the property.

There was a pickup parked right where I wanted to go, blocking the place where I wanted to stand. I walked around to the front of the old, tan Ford. I had intended to sneak a peek in the window of the bungalow to see if the closet door was closed. But as I passed the front of the truck, something reached out and grabbed my attention. I was surprised to see figures sitting in the cab. What was so startling is the fact that there hadn't been anyone sitting in there as I passed the truck door heading to the front of the vehicle. Now, what looked like two men—one with a beard and a plaid shirt, the other clean-shaven with coveralls—were sitting just as pretty as you please in the front seat of that truck. They looked like they were from very early in the 20th century, as both were wearing old-fashioned hats. More disconcerting was the fact that neither of them appeared to have eyes—just a flat blackness where their eyes should be—shark's eyes.

I spun and looked around at the foliage. I assessed the angle of the distant streetlights. I danced a little spastic jig in front of the truck. Up I jumped, waving my arms all around. I could see the shadows of my arms flailing about. It didn't affect the figures in the truck. I got the distinct impression they were amused. Their bodies were shaking slightly; I swear I could hear distant laughter. I looked to see where everyone else had gotten off to. They were all over at the door to *the* apartment. I looked back at the truck. The figures had departed. Panic set in.

My feet were glued to the spot. The inner voices screamed, "Run, you dope, run!" The icicles that were forming on my limbs froze me in place. My heart stopped for a moment. There was now a black dog sitting on the seat, its gaping maw visible just above the dashboard. It wasn't that malevolent chow Clevis kept locked up in his workshop. This was something far more heinous. The two men—well, their eyes were like flat dark splotches. This dog—its eyes were deep black hellish pits. They sucked light in.

The creature would become crystal clear for a moment and then almost fade into a dark cloud. The beast's black tongue lolled out of a mouth that offered a taste of hell here on earth. The dog was composed of layers of black—so many shades mingling together like maggots on three-day-old road kill. It wouldn't chew on your bones; it would gnaw on your soul. I wanted to run. My feet had failed me.

Then I heard Dave's voice cutting through the drone. I realized all I had been hearing was a buzzing that had grown louder and louder until it shut out anything else, underscored by a very unpleasant chuckling coming from the truck.

The dog stood up on the seat and gave a shake. It turned one last look my way, then walked off into nothingness. As the group approached I could finally take a step back, and I took a deep breath.

"I think I just saw the entity! Just a minute ago there were two guys in the cab of the old truck over there, then they changed into this black as tar hell hound. I'm sure I saw the thing that's causing all the problems."

"And it looked like a dog?" asked Dave.

"It might have *looked* like a dog, but that wasn't any dog. There was a horrid malevolent intelligence. It may not be a dog but that's how it manifested to me."

We had definitely kicked the hornets' nest. The buzzing kept getting louder. We walked over to make sure the closet door was open. I was worried that when we looked in the window there would be a really angry dead lady screaming at us. There was nothing as we peered through the window. We looked deeper toward the closet door. It was open.

We headed back toward the apartment. Having learned my lesson, I stuck with the group like glue. Isn't the guy who wanders off the first one to get it in those cheesy horror movies? We walked around to the back; we stopped in the space between the bungalow and the apartment.

Gwen looked concerned. "The energy here is getting very intense. I think we've worn out our welcome."

"Yeah I've seen all I need to tonight. I'd have to say the place is unquestionably haunted," Henry agreed.

We walked to the end of the apartment and turned the corner. Someone had stolen a piece of Oz's Emerald City; I'd be surprised if they hadn't dropped it into the garden behind the apartments. We stood there entranced by the spectacle that had bloomed among the twisted weeds, gnarled sticks, and debris. The garden had transformed into a glowing green snow globe. The insects flying into the sparkle would leave trails of flashing glitter. The light attracted more bugs; the air was alive with the flittering of wings. The surrounding high wall of trees and shrubs all neatly contained it on two of the sides. The apartments cordoned off the other luminescent boundaries. The top of the phenomenon was a tad bit higher than the two-story roofline.

The exception was the barrel-thick column in the center that reached far into sky, a spectral spotlight to the moon. Significantly more luminous than the surroundings, the pillar was alive with an unholy energy. Inside the swirling maelstrom of glowing smoke there was a constant sparkle punctuated by sporadic unearthly flashes. The pillar was coalescing, become more substantial. It was a phosphorescent vortex of epic proportions—to me, anyway. I broke the spell by speaking, for when the mind is dumbfounded the mouth will fire. "Darn, that's beautiful. I think we should really leave now."

Dave turned and looked dead at me. "Doesn't anyone want to take a walk in the garden?"

Everyone quickly turned and headed down the drive to the cars. As soon as my feet hit asphalt the buzzing subsided. I looked back toward the garden. Oz was still contained in the backyard, but I sure didn't want to be there when it spilled over. I think it took us about 30 seconds to get to my house. When we finally sat down in my living room Gwen was still shaking her head.

"That was a really screwed-up piece of property."

Dave agreed. "However, someone needs to help Penelope, and everything seems to be throwing us together to do this. Why else would your number appear like it did?"

"Maybe you just missed me." She seemed to reflect a bit. She took a deep breath. "I just wish we had some clearer direction to go on than what we're getting through Penelope from whatever this council of hers is. We really need to do something. We need to act. I get the feeling whatever it is, it is growing in size and influence."

I was idly flipping through the calendar section of the newspaper that sat on the coffee table in front of me. Even though I had read it, there was something I had missed. It was nebulous earlier, like the column of smoke in the garden. Now it hit me between the eyes. "Hey, amazing coincidence—look what I found. There's a psychic fair this weekend at the University Holiday Inn. Maybe we should seek an outside opinion on all this."

Henry balked a little. "I don't know that they can help us. What do they have to offer?"

Gwen stared at him with disdain. "They offer a different perspective. Your way is not the only way."

Dave diffused the situation with a grin and chuckle. "I think we should all go. The more, the merrier."

Chapter 12

The Psychic Fair

Black Eagle

The medicine path is a forced one. In order to learn we must be tricked. On the medicine path we are always fighting something, avoiding something, prepared for something; and that something is always unknown, greater, more powerful than we are. The unknown forces will come to you. Eventually, as time passes and you become accessible to power, you will get an ally, so there is nothing you can do now but to prepare yourself for the struggle. You will always struggle; it is our lot. So you must always prepare for the struggle that will come, for surely it will.

Robbie

Our neighbor Doug was there when Penelope and Dave showed up. Leigh and I invited him to go with us. We met Henry and Gwen in the parking lot. I had never been to a psychic fair. I certainly didn't know what to expect.

As we walked in through the double doors the reaction was instantaneous. The first medium had a table right in front of the doors. He looked at us very intently, then immediately dropped his head and stared at his hands in his lap. The body language was obvious. That's auspicious, I thought; the first sensitive wanted nothing to do with us.

Every other psychic in the room turned to look at us. With surreal, Bob Fosse choreography, all of their heads spun in perfect sync. There were about 30 or so of them; it was a comical sight. It wasn't a threatened reaction—just overwhelming curiosity. Maybe it was just my overactive imagination, as it was just for a split second, then everyone went back to what they were doing.

The main room was set up with three rows of seven small tables; there were six additional tables against the wall. Each one had a chair on either side. The tables were all covered with the effluvia of the arts. Runes and tarot cards were everywhere; the tables were covered with bright cloths and crystals. The smell of incense permeated the air, making my head spin. On the other two walls were tables of wares: books, talismans, ointments, and tapes. Dave suggested we split up to reconnoiter.

The seer's tables were mostly full. The distraught or just plain curious folks were packed in, seeing what the spirits had in store for them. Against one wall I noticed that one of the psychics kept looking at me with the most beatific smile. Her client, a heavyset woman in dark clothing, was sitting across from her in a scene of stark contradiction. Life apparently was not treating this woman fairly. The waves of despair just flowed off of her in strong tsunamis. Her body was quaking with each sob that spewed from her lips. But every time she looked down, her head bent with sorrow or digging for a Kleenex, the little redhead just turned and smiled at me. It was a blissful smile, filled with love you could feel. When the hurting woman across from her looked up, she shifted her attention back to her, offering solace.

I walked over to a table with a variety of books splayed across the top. I flipped through some interesting titles. Suddenly, I felt someone come up next to me, very close. I looked over to my left, and there stood the red-headed psychic. Her body was going through the motions of looking for a cassette. Her hands were flipping through the bins but her face was just beaming up at me. I glanced over my shoulder and saw that her client was still sitting at her table blowing her nose and sniffling. The psychic, however, was standing next to me smiling like it was all a grand game.

Leigh tapped my right shoulder and said, "We're going to go do the mini course."

When I looked back to my left, the psychic was back at her table with a cassette and comfort.

One of the amenities offered at a psychic fair is the "mini course." The different psychics show you how to see auras or read a palm or even teach you how to read tea leaves. This particular moment was the time allotted for the past-life regression session. We all sat down and tried to get comfortable. A fair number of people were in attendance for such a beautiful afternoon in Gainesville. The instructor came out, cleared his throat, and started his spiel.

Tall, thin, and balding, he began to work the crowd in a way that revealed he had done this many times. He started with a brief history of the past-life regression methodology, then we settled in to do the meditation. He dimmed the lights and started to walk us through the regression. Suddenly he began to falter. He tripped up on his words. What had started out as a well-rehearsed shamanic journey morphed into something completely different. It quickly became obvious that his relaxed and self-assured patter changed radically. The energy in the anteroom we were in grew preternatural. The poor guy kept trying to continue but was not having an easy time of it. He told everyone to envision a comfort place, a place where we felt safe. Somehow I ended up in the bathroom of our house. I've had some interesting occurrences in that bathroom so that's not the most relaxing place to go, but it's where my mind went.

Then the instructor started to really flub his words; he was having a bad time of it. I felt a striking chill envelop me. I opened my eyes; there in front of me in the empty chair was the dog—translucent, but very much there. The black pit exposed by its open mouth and lolling tongue struck my soul like an ice pick carved from obsidian. Its eyes were glowing black pits of despair. In my mind I could hear it laughing. Staring and laughing.

The instructor was now rushing through his presentation just trying to get done. He quickly brought everyone out of their various levels of trance. He started his return count. When he reached one, the dog slowly melted into black smoke and dissipated before my eyes. Everyone else started to stretch and rub their eyes, looking around groggily.

Leigh made a strange remark: "You know, it's funny: My safe place was the bathroom at home. That's not the most comfortable room in the house."

Gwen gave her a bemused look, "I've only been to your house a couple of times but that's where I went, too."

I looked around. "Anyone else?"

Henry, Doug, Dave—all of us had gone to my bathroom. Dave had seen a beautiful redhead at first and said he had seen her before in his dreams.

We walked outside to get some sunlight. As we sat outside the door, we talked about the experience so far and decided to kick it up a notch: One of us would get a reading.

"I don't care who gets the reading but you need to go to the short redhead. I can take a subtle hint. She keeps smiling at me. I think she wants to talk. No comment, Dave!"

"Penelope is the center of the activity. Shouldn't she go?" Gwen suggested.

Penny shrugged her shoulders. "Okay, I can go in. I'll get the 15-minute reading."

We sat and waited for 45 minutes. Penelope returned very reticent—shell-shocked. She looked like Bill the Cat, or maybe she had just wrapped a bare-wire electrical cord around her body and plugged it in. She was trying to assimilate all the info that had just been shown to her. She also was apparently trying to get the blood to start flowing again through her veins.

Gwen spoke up again to point out what should have been obvious. "Dave, this is your group. Maybe you should go get a reading."

"Okay. I'll go get a five-minute reading so you all don't have to wait too long. The 15-minute one was a killer. My foot went to sleep." He hobbled back into the building.

We waited 15 minutes for Dave to come back. When he did return he had the psychic in tow.

"I had to talk to the whole group," the redhead began, then turned and looked at me. "What took you so long? Y'all should have come right to me."

I stammered and mumbled, unable to form complete sentences as she continued.

"This land that you are concerned with has three ley lines crossing it. They all intersect at one point. And just to keep it fun let me tell you that they are all negative. What this group needs to do is change the polarity of the lines. That will give Penelope the relief she needs. Whatever nastiness that is there will have the source of its power cut off."

She continued with a grin and a giggle, almost like she was clucking. "Of course, y'all will need a good crystal to help power your ceremony. Focus your intentions."

She reached into her pocket to pull out a wonderful quartz crystal. It was 1/2 inch wide and 1 1/4 inches long. It glittered in her palm like a supernova. She stopped for a second; she slowly looked at each one in the group.

"No. Heavens no—this isn't going to work. I need to get you the big gun. Follow me."

We walked out to the parking lot, following her, to a white Pontiac. She popped open the back, exposing the packed trunk. She started to rummage through one of the big Tupperware bins that resided in there. When she had sunk her arm deep in she smiled wider and uttered a satisfied "a-ha."

She pulled out another quartz crystal. This one was 2 1/2 inches long and easily an inch wide. It was a little cloudy at the bottom but the top looked pretty clear. When she started to hand the crystal to Dave she yelped. We all looked at her hand, and her index finger had a 2-inch gash running down it. It started to bleed profusely.

"Oh, I do swear—I can't believe it. Look at this! What do they think they are doing!"? She licked her finger. "They really don't want y'all to have this. They don't want me to give it to you. Here. Take it!"

They? Lovely.

"Thank you so much. What do we owe you?" Dave politely asked.

The giggling had stopped; she eyed us with a serious look that could stop a clock. "Nothing. It's a gift. You'll need it."

She handed the crystal to Dave. He gave it the once-over, shook his head slightly, and handed it to me. There was not a single sharp edge on it, definitely not an edge that could draw blood. Yet there at the bottom of the "Big Gun," the psychic's blood was lightly smeared.

"You are going to have to clean the crystal of residual energies. The best way would be to soak it in seawater." She applied pressure to her finger and continued, "But in a pinch you can buy sea salt and soak it in water you dissolve the salts into."

A picture jumped into my head—a beautiful spring right on the Santa Fe River—and I asked, "Would spring water work?"

"Spring water will work, particularly if you draw the water right from the mouth of the spring where it exits from the earth. That would be absolutely perfect. It is especially effective if you went to the right spring to gather the water."

I knew instantly that Rum Island was the right spring. I don't know why; I just knew.

"Once you have cleaned the crystal you need to use it as the focal point of your intent. With that and the right invocation you should be fine. Let's see—I have an incantation here somewhere. Oh yes, say this." She made a theatrical pause and then continued:

"*We allow only the best and the highest to come through*
The white light protects us
And the violet light
Transmutes all negative energy into positive life-force
And we send it back to the cosmos with love."

She turned to Leigh and said, "You have a very powerful protector. You don't have anything to fear from any of this. If you were threatened, he would stop being involved to protect you." She glanced over at me. "However, he needs to be involved in this affair. Protection is being provided. Good luck!"

She gave each of us a big, long hug and said, "Stay strong, do not falter, and it will all work out."

David

Later that afternoon, after we had discussed plans for purifying the crystal, Henry and I were driving away when he suggested that we return to the psychic fair before it closed. When we showed up the fair was winding down. We wandered around looking at the tables full of wares. After the people had been herded out, the psychics all got together and approached us.

"The person you really want to speak with has left. He says he knows who and what you're dealing with. He wants nothing to do with it or you!'

Another of the group then spoke up. "Do you two realize we had to close the fair for a cleaning after you left? And now we'll have to stay here for at least an hour after you leave and clean it up again."

I looked over at our redhead. She looked like she was ready to burst out laughing. When the gathered group would say something particularly silly she would just roll her eyes.

Then they focused on Henry. "And you—you might think you're some kind of deep practitioner. You've been exploring a dark side that is way over your head. You need to stop now."

They looked at an ugly sore festering on Henry's forehead. He had had it for more than a year. It did not get better. "That sore on your forehead that just won't heal. I bet you've been to all kinds of specialist and no one can figure out what it is. Am I right?"

Henry started to stammer, "We...I...I just haven't figured if it's cancer or just a fungus."

"Until you get your head screwed on straight that wound on your forehead will *never* heal. It is a spiritual affliction. Your mortal soul is oozing out of your body through that sore."

I cracked up—out loud and hard—when they told him this. They gave me a very stern look; I shrugged my shoulders. Then it was my turn to talk. "Don't be such tough guys. If you think you had a difficult time cleaning up after us, just imagine what it must be like to deal with what we are dealing with every day. So we sullied your little affair with nasties. We are going to have to fight and defeat them soon. I don't see any of you brave enough to join in."

The tall, balding man whose dog and pony show we interrupted earlier asked us to leave at that point.

Robbie

Leigh went to work at Shands Teaching Hospital on the U.F. Campus the Monday morning after the fair. One of her colleagues cornered her in the hall.

"What was up with you and that group you were with this weekend?"

Leigh was caught off guard. He continued, "I was at the psychic fair. When you and your friends walked in, every psychic in the room turned and looked at you all."

She deftly deflected his inquiry. "Well, we live in a haunted house and had some questions. Did you enjoy your trip there?"

After hearing this, it occurred to me that we may be a force to be reckoned with. Maybe we did have a chance. I sure hoped we had a chance. Time was running out. I felt like Dorothy watching the sand drain from the wicked witch's hourglass. And we sure weren't in Kansas anymore.

Chapter 13

The Shotgun House

Black Eagle

I am compelled to teach you to *see*. I am compelled, therefore, to teach you to feel and act as a warrior. To *see* without first being a warrior would make you waifish and weak; it would give you a false meekness—a desire to retreat; your body would decay because you would become indifferent. It is my personal commitment to make you a warrior so you won't crumble.

A warrior should be prepared only to do battle. His spirit is not geared to indulging and complaining, nor is it geared to winning or losing. The spirit of a warrior is geared only to struggle, and every struggle is a warrior's last battle on earth. Thus the outcome matters very little to him. In his last battle on earth a warrior lets his spirit flow free and clear. A warrior lives for this struggle. And as he wages his battle, knowing that his *will* is impeccable, a warrior laughs and laughs.

Robbie

It was late afternoon when Dave arrived. Crossing Sixth Street in front of my home, successfully dodging the plethora of traffic common at this time of day, we headed over to Samantha's on foot. There was an old, abandoned hovel on the bend of her road—a faded white shotgun shack. It had been empty since I had lived in the area. The scrub hadn't reclaimed it yet; I think one of the neighbors occasionally cut the yard just to keep it semi-respectable. It had always given me the creeps when I walked by.

There was a beautiful blue sky; the smell of fall was in the air. A nice autumn day in Florida means it was still in the upper 80s. This time, however, walking past the house was different. When we got right in front of the house, I broke out in goose bumps. The hair on the back of my neck stood up. My body was in full fear mode. There was no visible reason for it. I stopped and looked around. There was absolutely nothing to be afraid of that I could see.

Dave turned around to look at me. He noticed something was bugging me right away. "All of a sudden my body feels really afraid. I'm not afraid but I sure have all the physical signs," I said.

There was that knowing snicker. He said, "You'll have to get used to that. It's one of the ways to tell when there are energies around you. Something with this house is getting stronger—really more pronounced. When the spirit leaves, or we leave its area of influence, you'll feel the sensations dissipate."

As we got around the corner and past the driveway the feelings gradually faded away. By the time we got to Samantha's house I couldn't feel it anymore.

When we asked about the house we got a sad story. When she first moved in, there was a real old couple that lived there. They had moved in right after the war and had been there ever since.

They passed away; it had to have been within weeks of each other. Their son moved in, but he kept mostly to himself. Then one night he walked out on to the front sidewalk and put both barrels of a shotgun in his mouth. It was quite a mess. Samantha didn't know who owned it now. She explained, "They've never put it up for sale. They had tenants there a couple of times but no one ever stays for long."

When we walked back to my house the feelings were there but not nearly as strong—present, but much more fleeting. In fact, they were downright ghostly.

When we arrived at my house Penelope was waiting there with her bicycle. It was disturbing; she was just waiting in the yard, waiting for us to get there.

As we approached she called to us, "Sorry, guys. Clevis phoned today and was furious. He said he's done playing around. If you come to the property again he'll call the cops. He said if you keep pushing your luck, it will be worse. He was threatening to send his guardians after you."

Dave laughed. "I don't think he's actually in control of that hoard any longer. Nice try at a scare, but I think they are already coming at us. We've seen what we needed. How about you? What did he say to you?"

"He just asked when I would be coming back. He tried to convince me that it was you all that had everything all wound up. I really wasn't comforted; I was more creeped out. He did assure me everything there was just friendly and I really shouldn't be afraid. I still don't think I will be going back."

"No," said Dave, still cackling. "I would wait until Hell freezes over before I would spend a night in that house again if I were you."

Dave

Stephanie dropped by in the afternoon as I was in my yard talking to Carol, my next door neighbor, about all the things associated with Penelope's demon. Carol was studying psychology at U.F.; she was also interested in the occult. She planned to be a counselor after she graduated.

Stephanie was into music. She had a great voice; she would often sing, no matter where she happened to be. She always called me Uncle Dave, as did many of the girls who lived in the student ghetto. I was a bit older than them, so I had become something of a father figure, I guess. When they needed something fixed, I would look at it. If there was trouble in the neighborhood, I took care of it.

Stephanie was a bit eccentric. She was an earth mama type, always smelling of patchouli and always dressed in flowing sundresses—that sort of garb. She also fancied herself as a witch—a good witch.

I went over all the details of the situation at Clevis's property. Stephanie expressed a keen interest in getting involved.

"Listen, Stephanie. This whole deal isn't your typical Tarot party or Ouija board session. There is something heinous involved in this, and it's dangerous. I will have to think about it. I also need to talk it over with the other people involved before I can bring you in. Also, you need to really think about what you are getting into."

"I know what I'm doing."

"Let me get back to you. It's not my decision alone. There are others involved in this. A team and how they work together is paramount to success or failure. I am too young to die yet."

"Well, the offer stands."

"I'll get back to you. It's getting dark. Let me walk you home."

On the way back from Stephanie's house, I took a shortcut between a row of houses. I found a pile of rubbish lying near one of the old houses. There I saw something I needed to use to teach Robbie a valuable lesson. I picked it out of the trash and took it home with me.

Robbie

Dave handed me the dirty chair leg and asked, "So what do you think?"

"I don't know. What should I think?"

"Just sit and feel it. What kind of vibe does the high chair leg give you? I got it at a crime scene."

"Oh, man. The mother killed the baby, didn't she?"

Visions of Antoine Dietz's painting "Hunger, Madness, Crime" popped into my head, except the child was sitting in the chair, face all bloated, a portrait of gray and blue.

"She strangled the kid in the chair, didn't she? Thanks, Dave. What am I supposed to do with this?"

Dave was being very coy. "You need to learn how to deal with this kind of energy, Robbie. You need to figure out what is going on here."

The leg threw off a horrible vibe. I tried to put up walls to protect myself, but every time I got around it my mind flashed on the horrible scene of the child in the chair—the mother just rocking away, eyes burning with madness. It tried to haunt me; I had trouble keeping it in check. No matter what I did, I could not remove the twisted visions seared into my mind. Like a sick, warped ballet, the scene unfolded over and over again of a hysterical mother strangling her baby.

A week had passed. Dave was over, being his ever-cheerful self. "Let me see that creepy high chair leg I gave you."

"Here. Hopefully you'll take it back."

"Did it give you problems?"

"What do you think? It came from a crime scene—psycho mother killed her baby. Pretty screwed up, don't you think?"

"Robbie, I picked it up from a trash pile by the side of the road."

"*What*?"

"I have no idea where this insignificant chunk of wood came from. I did tell you it came from a crime scene. The truth is I took it from a garbage pile on the side of the road near my house. You see, you turned it into an artifact all by yourself.

"Learn to discern, be careful not to let yourself be led! If you had truly listened, you would have known better. It only took a few key words and you took it to grand levels! Your sense of self-importance convinced you it had to be something special. I would never give you something insignificant. Oh god, that was good!"

Dave was laughing hard. He had tears running down his cheeks, and his body shook.

"Buzz off!"

"Just remember the lesson," he wheezed between gasps for air.

I would never forget it.

Chapter 14

Cleaning the Crystal

David

You have got to stop talking to yourself. Every one of us does that. We carry on an internal conversation with ourselves. We talk about our world. We talk about fishing and hunting. The simple fact is we maintain our world with our internal jabber. Whenever we finish talking to ourselves the world is always as it should be. We renew it; we rekindle it with life; we uphold it with our internal chatter. Not only that, but we also choose our paths as we talk to ourselves. Thus we repeat the same choices over and over until the day we die, because we keep on repeating the same internal talk over and over until the day we die.

This whole affair with the chair leg demonstrates it. A warrior is aware of this. He strives to stop his talking. This is the last point you have to know if you want to live like a warrior. You have to know when to be—and not talk.

Robbie

I knew the water we would need to cleanse the crystal would come from the spring at Rum Island. I don't know why Rum Island; I just knew it deep in my soul.

The Santa Fe River is one of those black water Southern rivers. Due to the density of the cypress trees and palmettos that line the river and because it meanders at such a slow pace, it is exceptionally dark. It's the major tributary of the Suwannee River. The other amazing thing about the Santa Fe is how many natural springs feed the flow. Some like Rum Island and Ginnie Springs are right on the river. Some holes, like Blue Springs, have small separate runs before they empty in. The river flows out of Lake Santa Fe, and a little ways outside of High Springs it drops into a sinkhole only to come back out of the ground 3 miles later.

The remote, sparsely populated areas that the river runs through allow for an abundance of wildlife. Bear, deer, wild pigs, and gators are common. If you're really lucky you catch a glimpse of an otter, a bald eagle, a Florida panther, or even a skunk ape. That's the Florida Sasquatch.

Rum Island is a Columbia County park on the north bank of the river. It's the party place of the true locals: the farmer and his family who come down to the swimming hole, the bikers from the bar on the main road, the fellows who hunted the area in the wintertime and stumbled on it, or just the preacher and his kin after a sweaty sermon on Sunday morning. On weekdays, because it was way off the beaten trail, down a bunch of dirt backroads, no one would be there. It was perfect.

I picked up Penelope in the morning. It was still early but I was in a hurry. The lightning storms had come back with a vengeance, and I wanted to be out of the water before the thunder started booming. It's a fair piece of road to Rum Island from Gainesville. You go out past High Springs, but instead of the southern route out of town you head to the northwest. After you cross the river, take the first left, and you step back in time: scattered homesteads, an outhouse or two, miles of fields, and pastures all interspersed with thick stands of oak, magnolia, dogwoods, and pine. And the cows—everywhere there are the cows.

Most of the time I had gotten to Rum Island from the river; luckily I had also driven there a few times. There were no signs advertising its whereabouts—not even a little county park arrow. Nothing. You turn left between the two pastures after you pass the farm with the red barn. It was a strip of white sand that headed off toward the woods in the distance. There was no street sign. However, there were no signs telling you that you couldn't go down it, either.

The first time down the road can be unnerving. The pines gradually give way to towering cypress trees and primeval oaks. The moss hangs thicker and thicker the farther down the road you go. All of a sudden there's a trailer with a bunch of pickup trucks tucked back in the palmettos right in front of you. It's takes you by surprise. For a minute it seems like it's a driveway. Out in the sticks, lots of people have long driveways. But no, the road continues to curve off to the right and the underbrush gets deeper on both sides, with cypress and palm becoming the dominant trees. It was damper than usual due to all the storms we had been having. I was really hoping that the sound of "Dueling Banjos" didn't come through the trees from some distant abode.

A couple more turns then we were able to see the river. Way out there, the local legends say the island was the location of a still during prohibition, and it certainly could have been true. It sure is remote enough; back in the day there was a lot of bootleg whiskey coming north out of Florida. Looking out the car window I noticed that the river was much closer to us than it had been before.

The scenery changed more. Rather than a thick stand of trees and brush lining the road, on either side of the car was swamp. The road is raised above the marsh, so we were able to make it to the park. If we got another heavy rain, travel would be severely limited.

The road opened up to an area with concrete picnic tables and big oaks that provided adequate shade for a day at the swimming hole. I knew there would be no one there because it was in the middle of the week, but there was a second reason why the park was empty: The river was inches short of full flood stage. All the low-lying areas around the park were underwater. There was a natural rim around the edge of the spring and the park area was elevated, but the immediate surroundings to it were submersed.

The wildlife in Florida can be dangerous but it's normally benign (cottonmouths don't count). There are very few times animals maliciously attack for no reason. Of course if they are hungry, or the rivers are in flood stage, all bets are off. This was one of those times. The critters that lived near the river were now all homeless. For some reason, that makes them angry. The snakes and the gators are swimming around, not happy about Mother Nature's little gift of abundant water. Did I mention the moccasins? They already have an attitude, and now they're irritated.

The peninsula was nice and dry above the water, but the spring that was normally on the edge of the channel was now part of the river. There is the Devil's Eye Spring. It sits in the Santa Fe but the volume of the flow keeps the immediate surrounding water crystal clear. Where the flow weakens, the black water and the clear water slowly blend. That was not the case here. At Rum Island, the floodwater was completely obscuring the springhead. Oh boy—that nice, inviting, dark brown, tannic water, beckoning to me, flowing darker now with the added density of the stirred-up bank debris and mud. There was still enough separation that the spring pool had formed a little eddy. In the middle of the eddy was a large, floating log, about 20 feet in length.

Diving into a flooded river is not the brightest thing in the world to do. Still, it needed to be done, and Rum Island had to be the place. So, after surveying the situation, I spun the car around, about 50 feet from the spring, put it into park, and turned off the engine. It was country quiet. You could hear the birds and the trickle of the water. You could hear the breeze in the trees. Luckily, it had warmed up enough that I wasn't going to freeze after the initial shock. The river water was always much warmer than spring water. I left the keys in the ignition and the doors of the car open; one of the advantages of being way out in the boonies is there is no one to watch out for. I threw my shoes on the floor of the driver's side and my shirt on the seat. From the back I gathered my mask and fins, and a big, old, empty, glass gallon bottle. I also grabbed a small handful of tobacco.

I walked down to the edge of the spring; I asked the spirits for permission to get some water to purify the crystal. I knew this was the water that was destined to do the task. I sprinkled the offering into the water and gave a prayer of thanks to all the spirits of the area. Not hear any resounding nays, I felt that permission was given, perhaps begrudgingly. I put on my snorkeling gear and proceeded to the edge of the water.

Penelope sat down at the picnic table that was closest to the spring. I waved and slowly lowered myself into the pool. The initial shock wasn't as bad as usual, thanks to the warmer river water. It took all my nerve to swim out into the middle of the pool. You couldn't see your hands once they went into the murky water. I swam out to the center, took a big breath through my snorkel, and down I dove.

After about 6 feet, the water started to clear. At the mouth of the spring, the water was clear like tap water. All around me I could see the impenetrable river—brown, dark. At the spring mouth, about 14 feet down, is a little fissure in the floor of the pool 2 feet long by 8 inches wide. That, with several other auxiliary holes, gave it a fair flow. At the hole where the water first flowed out of the earth, I took the lid off the jar, burped the air out, filled it up, and resealed the jar. All the time I had kept a running commentary in my mind thanking the spirits, telling myself that the gators and snakes weren't going to get me—giving myself a thin veneer of courage. Then it all went dead quiet. Even that constant rushing sound you get when you're under water in a river. Dead quiet.

The voice was as clear as day: "You got it. Now GET OUT!!"

I don't know how I didn't take a full breath of water right then and there. I shot to the surface, spat out the snorkel, and gasped a big gulp of air. As fast as I could, with a big jar of water under my arm, I swam toward shore. If I could have walked on water I would have; I would have *run*. The shore looked to be a lot farther away than it did when I swam out to the spring mouth. In fact, the whole spring pool seemed to have grown a lot bigger. And now I wanted badly to exit, posthaste. I was panicked. I wanted to be out of that water; I didn't want anything grabbing me and keeping me there. I was quivering as bad as a turkey on Thanksgiving.

The log was floating between me and the shore. I knew the futility of my next act, but I had to get out of the water. I jumped up on top of the log like a lumberjack—well, more like a lumberjack in swim fins and a mask, carrying a gallon glass jar of pristine spring water. The log threw me at the edge. I tried to walk on the water but, as I mentioned before, couldn't. As I fell I made sure to protect the jar. I wasn't worried about hitting my head on a rock, but I wasn't going to go back for more water.

I pulled myself out of the pool, flopping around like a wounded seal. I waddled over to the bench where Penelope was sitting. I sat down, set down the jar, and took off my mask and fins. After taking a few deep breaths, my composure began to return. I took the jar of water over to the car and put it safely in the back seat. I grabbed some more tobacco and then went back down to the edge of the spring to thank the spirits for allowing me to get the water.

While I was squatting down on the bank, Penelope started to say my name like a chant—soft, then louder and louder. After the fifth "Robbie," it turned into a panicked scream. "Run. Run *now*!"

I turned; Penelope was already bolting for the car. My composure was shot, just like my nerve. I started screaming back to her.

"What?! What?!!!"

Failing to get a reply, I ran as fast as I could to the car. I grabbed my mask and fins off of the picnic table as I scrambled past in my harried flight. The whole time Penelope was freaking out.

She just kept yelling, "Hurry! Hurry! He's coming! Hurry!"

I threw the swim gear in the back. I jumped in the open door, started the car, and peeled out of the parking lot, spraying mud and gravel everywhere. I didn't have to close my door; the momentum of the ride slammed it shut. We flew down that dirt road like the devil was on our tail.

All the while Penelope was chanting, "Go! Go!"

My heart was pounding. My driving would have put the Dukes of Hazzard to shame. I was channeling the spirit of an old bootlegger running his load from Rum Island. We fled, and we fled *fast*.

When we got to a long, straight section of road between two big pastures I stopped. I got out of the car and plopped down in the soft white sand. I tried to catch my breath. As I soaked up the sun, my heart started to slow down.

Penelope was still wide eyed—very frightened. I had to know: "What was that all about?"

"When you walked back down to the water, an Indian floated up out of the spring. He looked really angry and wanted you gone. When he had completely risen out of the water he started to come at you. That's when I yelled."

I lay there in the sun for at least 30 minutes before I could put on my shoes and shirt and even think about moving on. We finally headed home with the water we so desperately needed. I was grateful that the price had not been too dear.

"So you didn't actually finish saying thank you. Properly that is. You know you have to go back," Dave said, obviously amused.

"Ah, no. I don't quite see that happening."

"It will be soon." He winked at me. "You'll know when the time is right. At least a swarm of flying monkeys didn't swoop down on you."

"If they had, Dave, I would still be driving!"

It was dark. I really couldn't tell if it was a moonless night or not. The storms had broken up enough that I could see the random groups of stars scattered about. The rain had enhanced all of the smells of the night air. The pastures wafted up a clean greenness.

As I got to the big bend, the deeper scents of the heavy woods came through. My headlights lit up the front of the trailer there. They were probably used to the occasional midnight dalliance down at the water. None of that tonight—not with the flood waters present. I couldn't see it, but as I got closer to the river I could smell it. I knew I had reached the point where, beyond the little strip of road I was driving on, there was deep water.

The park had less space to turn around in now. I turned the car so I wouldn't have to worry about doing it in a hurry in the pitch black. As the headlights flashed out across the river, spring, and surrounding forest, I scanned for the glow of eyes. I felt a little better when there were none. No flying monkeys tonight! I got out and gave my eyes a chance to adjust. There were a few frogs making their calls, but most of the night noise was muffled in the distance.

There were enough stars to let me perceive the outline of the treetops. I could see where the rim of the springs was; the rocks were whiter than the rest of the area. I walked toward the spring and found a place right where the rocks started. I did not plan to get wet that night! That left me with a very narrow bit of ground to balance on.

I gave offerings of tobacco to all directions, including the sky above and earth below. I lit up a bundle of sweet grass as a gift. I thanked the spirits for the water they had magnanimously provided. The dark and quiet was comforting; I felt relaxed. My thanks had been accepted.

It was getting quieter but it wasn't getting darker. My eyes were adjusting really well. The trees were all covered with phosphorescence. It wasn't the nasty green; it was a bright, silvery white. Glowing suits of light surrounded all the trees. I was able to look around and see every tree distinctly, each one unique in its glow. I gazed up at the sky—still no moon.

Across the spring to the northwest a light started to coalesce. A smoky, swirling white mist was forming that was getting thicker and thicker. It cleared in the center. It was a white doorway into the woods. It wasn't the woods I was in. I froze.

My mind raced. I didn't think I could walk on water. I wasn't going to try to swim over there. Was it a gift or a trap? I couldn't figure it out. I wanted to check it out, but my rational mind was screaming. I didn't feel threatened. Penelope had been pretty scared, though. In the end the rational mind put up too much of a fight; fear is a wicked foe. I tried to retreat in a more dignified manner that time, but my tail was still between my legs.

"You missed a fantastic opportunity!" Dave was always so cheerful in the face of utter disaster.

"I didn't see it that way."

"It is because you didn't see. You were offered a fabulous gift. That portal may have taken you anywhere you wanted to go. Instead, you beat foot out of there. I bet the spirits were laughing at your exit.

"Maybe fortune will pay you a visit in the future. But a repeat of such a gift is rare. They truly took a shining to you. By the way, I need to take the crystal out to Gwen's place."

Dave

The next day I rode out to Gwen's house with the crystal Robbie had given me safely tucked away in a small leather bag. I wanted to see what kind of power it had. Gwen was waiting for me outside when I got there.

"Did you bring the crystal with you?"

"Got it right here. Interesting stone. I can't believe it cut the medium when she gave it to us."

"I can't, either. That doesn't bode well."

Gwen and I set the crystal up in her dining area, a table just off the kitchen; we sat with it between us. For several hours we manipulated it, getting different colors to emit from it throughout the course of the afternoon. It was apparent to us both that the crystal was rather special; it contained a significant amount of power. As afternoon turned into evening, we halted our testing. We discussed the case in more detail. Gwen wanted to know particulars of how I got involved in the case and what exactly had happened up to that point. I spent the next hour filling her in on the details.

When I finished, she sat silent for a moment, then she said something peculiar: "The demon is going to get at you through Penelope. It is going to go after you in a way that you would never suspect. No specifics—I just know it will try to enter you. You are the biggest threat to it at the moment. If something happens to you, the rest of the group will fall apart. Be very careful. Expect anything. The feeling is very strong."

I had no sooner gotten home than my phone rang. It was Penelope.

"Do you have the crystal?" she asked.

"Yes."

"Please come over and bring it with you."

"I can come by tomorrow afternoon. It's late, and I need some sleep."

"Come by at 4. Bring the crystal with you. It's important."

Things seemed to be getting weirder and weirder. What on earth did Penelope want with the crystal? Gwen's words raced through my mind. The demon would use Penelope to get at me. What made it even more bizarre was that I knew that, for the most part, Penelope had been reluctant to even hold the crystal for long. I guess I would know when I got to her hotel room. Sometimes I miss fear.

It was nearly 4 p.m. when I pulled up in front of her room. She answered the door on the first knock. She was dressed in a bathrobe. She had a distant look in her eyes. It was a scene out of *Ghostbusters*. I was beginning to feel like the Keymaster....

"Do you have the crystal?" When I nodded, she continued, "Let me have it please. Henry and I need to use it."

I handed her the crystal, curious now as to what she was up to. There was incense burning—frankincense, if I was not mistaken. There was a bowl of herbs sitting on the nightstand by her bed. It gave me the impression of a mock altar of sorts. I even saw a mandrake root. She held the crystal up to the light, examined it for a second, and smiled. She then set it on the nightstand, turned, and kissed me. I was so taken off guard I didn't have time to react. I was suddenly intoxicated, drifting into a state where everything was like a dream. Sirens began going off in my head. I knew something was very wrong, but I couldn't break free of the spell I was under.

Gwen's voice was screaming in my head: "The demon will use Penelope to get into you!"

I walked right into a trap!

"Don't leave. We have just started." She smiled a wicked smile.

"I know what you are, and you will *not* get me!"

I didn't stop until I reached my house. The phone was ringing when I walked into my apartment.

Robbie wanted the crystal for the cleansing. He seemed to notice something was up with me, but didn't come out and say anything directly.

I hung up the phone realizing that Gwen had been right. The demon wanted me and had attacked me in a way I never expected. Had I not broken free, I wonder what would have happened. Whatever it was, it couldn't have been good. I made a mental note to be doubly on guard from that point forward. My slip had almost cost me the entire battle. It would not happen again.

Several nights later, there was a frantic knocking at my door. I looked out, and there was Henry's old van. I opened the door of my duplex to let him in. If he hadn't been walking I would have sworn he was dead. He was more washed out than normal.

"They were right, you know? You and I got all in their face, but they were right."

"Henry, sit down man. Take a deep breath. Who was right?"

"The psychics said we were in over our head. They were right; I'm done with this whole thing. If you know what's best for you, you'll drop it, now! You have no idea."

"What happened? I thought you were all for this. Are you succumbing to the enemy fear? Is it that bad?"

"Dave, you don't even know."

I was sure I knew where this was going, "Come on. What could be so horrible it could scare you? The Great and Powerful Lokison?"

"Your sarcasm doesn't help. You weren't there. It started innocent enough. I wanted to try some of the exercises I had been reading about."

"No gloating. What scared you?"

"It was really late last night; I mean 1 or 2 a.m. I heard a knock on the door. I thought it was you or Doug. When I opened the door Penelope was there. She was looking...radiant. I asked her how she had gotten there she just smiled and laughed. I invited her in. She swept into the room; she was different. She told me how she felt we had been progressing with the crystal. She felt she wouldn't be needing as much help as we thought.

"She looked at me and said, 'All because of you and that wonderful crystal' and then she leaned over and gave me a big hug. 'Can I see it before we fill it again with more magic?'"

I said 'Penelope, why didn't you bring it with you? I left it with you, didn't I?' She grinned a wicked grin, then she said, 'That's right. Silly me. Much easier this way, anyway.'"

This was getting uncomfortably familiar, I thought.

I looked at Penelope. She headed back to my room. I followed; I don't think I had a choice. Her words were intoxicating. But then she said, 'So this is Henry's little shack. How quaint.'

"'Wait,' I said. 'You've been here before.'

"'Have I, little man?'

"I swear I couldn't move. I felt like a mouse hypnotized by a swaying cobra. I glanced down; her fingers ended in black talons. I mean, it was beautiful in a sick sort of way, with the hands like those of the undead and all. She brought her mouth close to mine and breathed heavily. It wasn't intoxicating anymore. It was fetid, like a charnel house. She smelled of rotting corpses."

"She went on to tell me, 'If the crystal were here I would need some cooperation from you but since it's not I think I'll just take as I need.' Well, then she grabbed me by the throat and laughed. Her free hand grabbed me and then she picked me up. It wasn't pleasant; it hurt. She slammed me onto the bed. I felt little hands hold me down spread-eagle. I tried to get away but I was stuck fast to the mattress. She ripped her skin off. I could see flecks of wet hair where skin used to be. She didn't bleed; she oozed. Her teeth had grown long and sharp. When she smiled it was horrific, especially with the flesh sloughing off of her face. I started to gag. I turned my head and closed my eyes. I heard a thousand voices start to laugh."

"Then this thing says, 'I thought you might not be a man about this' and I felt two hands reach out from the bed and spin my head up. Penelope, or whatever it was, leaned in closer. I felt her hot breath on my face. Two talons pulled my eyelids open. She then took a sharp toothpick and propped open my lids so I couldn't close them. Then she says, 'I could just force you to watch, but this is much more gratifying.' As she took care of the other eye, she says, 'This way if it is too much for you to bear, you can still close your eyes, little man who fancies himself as a sorcerer. I won't stop you. It will be fun to see if the toothpicks break or if you just pierce the lids.' I thought I was dead for sure!"

I was thanking my lucky stars I had narrowly avoided that aspect of the demon.

"A musk smell filled the room that was repellent and exotic at the same time. I can't repeat the gory details." Henry looked down at his feet and said in a near whisper, "The worst part of it is, she ripped the Band-Aid off my forehead."

I was hoping this story would end soon.

"I felt totally weak. I lay there in what was once skin and was now turning to an ectoplasmic goo. I'm still disgusted thinking about it."

"You know that wasn't Penelope, right, Henry?"

"I don't care if it was her or her fairy godmother. I am done—d-o-n-e, done! And you should be, too!"

"I can't do that, Henry. I am a warrior."

Robbie

Penelope dropped off the crystal in its new, hand-sewn, blue satin pouch. It was a rock, but it had changed. It was heavier—cloudier—than it had been when we had received it. I wasn't sure what the others had done but the stone needed a cleaning bad. The moon would be bright, so I figured I could just put the crystal in the spring water and leave it out in the moonlight overnight.

I found a Leigh-crafted stoneware chalice to put the crystal in. As night fell, I went out to the front stoop. I set the chalice where it would get full exposure to the moon all night. As I thanked the spirits of the springs and the water, I filled the glass full.

I looked up into the star-filled sky. It was a clear, calm night; I was thinking that this should work just fine. Because I had experienced the interesting play with the wind, I thought I would ask for assistance. As I petitioned for help from the four winds, my hair lifted slightly. I felt the faintest tickle on my face. It could be a confirmation or my imagination. I turned, entering the house so I could go to bed.

The floor shaking violently jacked me up out of a peaceful slumber. It was then I realized that it wasn't daylight; the bright flashes were hellish lightning. The wind roared through the open bedroom window, causing the curtains to stand out straight from the walls flapping like a battle flag. The sound of the rain pelting down on the roof was deafening. I hurriedly closed the window and lay back down. The storm had come up out of nowhere. The weather report earlier, before I went to bed, made no mention of the tempest howling outside. I went back to sleep listening to the noise of the wind and rain. I awoke a few hours later, got up, and opened the window. The moon was shining brightly through a cloudless sky. I closed the window so I couldn't have been dreaming about the storm.

When I got up in the morning, I went out front. The chalice with the crystal was still there. It had rained overnight, the grass was still wet, and you could smell it in the air. The rock was sitting lower in the glass. I gently lifted the crystal up out of the water. It had changed rather dramatically. I was shocked that it felt denser yet lighter. It was both shorter and thicker. I looked through the crystal; to my amazement it was clear. Now, all of the fissures, all of the cloudiness, all of the flaws were gone. There was something left, though—something that didn't reveal itself until then. If you looked at the bottom of one of the facets, the portrait of a werewolf stood out in relief. That's what it looked like to me, and when I showed this to the others they all agreed. The spirit of the crystal had fully manifested and was ready to help.

It was showtime.

Chapter 15

The Devil Dog and Ella

David

Only by acting can one become a medicine man. This whole affair with Penelope and her demon is no accident. You were chosen for this. Power reached out and tapped you upside the head, like a brick in a sock. You now have the absolute need to live like a warrior. If you fail, you will die; it is really that simple. The look on your face right now is hysterical. If I had a camera I would capture that look to hang up in my living room.

There is no need for us to say anything about Henry or the others. It's silly to try to force people to agree with us. We shouldn't try to impose our will when people don't behave the way we want them to. The worst thing one can do is confront human beings bluntly. A warrior proceeds strategically. If one wants to stop our fellow companions, we must always be outside the circle that presses them. From outside the circle we can focus the pressure, not just respond to it.

We have a real demon on our hands. This is a rare occurrence, my friend. As time passes, I am becoming keenly aware of how powerful and insidious this demon is. Remember this: Fright never injures anyone. What injures the spirit is having someone always on your back, beating you, and telling you what to do and what not to do. Just make sure the demon doesn't jump on your back. Essentials are what warriors deal with. People hardly ever realize that we can cut anything from our lives, any time, just like that. They are nothing—nothing at all if we want to drop them. They have no essence in the end. Only one thing is indispensable for anything we do in this matter, and that is spirit. One can't do without the spirit. Without spirit, we are already dead meat.

Robbie

Penelope rode her bike over to my house for a visit. She had taken to riding her bike because, more and more, these grinning faces would pop up in front of her. They would stick out their tongues, constantly taunting her. They were making it very hard to drive.

She came in and sat down. With the front door ajar and the double doors open to the music room, it seemed even more spacious than usual. I even had the French doors to the Florida room open. That was a room with three walls of glass. Because it was shaded, there were no window treatments. The bright light flooded out to the living room. It was a wonderful, relaxing space.

Penelope was seated in a chair looking across the living room into the Florida room. She was very skittish. When our roommate, Crystal, dropped something in the hall, Penelope almost jumped out of her skin. She and I spoke for a bit, as Crystal was getting ready for work.

"Even today as I came over here, I passed a tree and—boom—a face would pop out from behind it. It makes it very hard to ride the bike. Or worse, I see the spirits that I saw when Clevis's grandfather was taking me out of my body. They just sit there and taunt me. Well, they don't sit there; they float along with me. Sometimes I'll look down into the basket and there will be a head in it. Then the head turns and makes the most horrible faces, like they're made of rubber. The teeth get long and sharp. Then other faces appear floating all around me. They start to taunt me. I can't even repeat some of the vile things they say. It is revolting and disturbing." She fidgeted with her graying locks.

"The faces they make I can't describe. I'm surprised my heart hasn't just stopped right there and then. Usually before the actual heart attack starts, these big Native American spirits show up. When they're there the spirits and faces run away, most of the time. Sometimes—I wish I knew why—they don't help at all! Either they won't or can't. If it's at night, that night usually becomes an awful night. The spirits won't let me sleep. Sometimes even—" Her face suddenly drained of color, and her eyes widened. "Turn slow and look over your left shoulder, in the Florida room."

I thought ghosts and things are supposed to be creatures of the night. I turned; I saw it, too. The demon dog was sitting there. It was a bright, cloudless Florida day. Brilliant sunshine was flooding the room we were staring into; the dog was just sitting there, pretty as you please. Though it appeared to be translucent, it was definitely there nonetheless, smiling malevolently at us. Its eyes were pits of darkness, like wells to Hell. Well, not really dark—more like a lack of light, and lack of dark as well. They were just pits of nothing. A vortex. They were deep, and you could get sucked right in.

I could hear, at least in my head, the two ghosts in the house. The male was blubbering something, and the crazy female was screaming incoherently. I was freaked out. I could feel the spirits in the house and they were freaking out. "Penny, what exactly do you see there?"

"It's a big dog. But that's not right. I—no—I've seen that thing before but right now it's a big dog. You can see it, right?"

"Oh yeah. I've seen that dog before! Why is it in here?"

Its amused contempt was weighing on me like an anvil. Emanating from it was more and more pure evil, consuming waves of hatred that washed over us like the steady stream of a gutter during a heavy rain. There it sat, in the beautiful bright sunshine, tongue lowly out, panting, glaring, scaring the life out of us.

Crystal came out of her bedroom and said, "Okay, I'm off to work. Oh, what are you two up to? Are you talking that ghost hooey again? You know none of that exists."

I figured, you know, maybe let's find out. It was experiment time. I said, "Crystal, you don't see anything? Like maybe over there in the Florida room?"

She marched straight across the floor and into the middle of the little room I was pointing at. She marched right through the dog. It wavered, then was right there in front of her.

"I don't know what you two are talking about there is absolutely nothing in here." She walked back effortlessly through the dog. "There is no such thing as a ghost! You are all just seeing things. This is getting creepy. I need to go to work. Bye-bye!"

As soon as Crystal left I went to the telephone and called Dave.

"Reitz Union Productions. Dave speaking."

"I have a big problem."

"You've just been playing with it too much. Take a breather, give it a rest, and in a little while it'll come back."

"Not funny."

"You are a little young for that problem, though."

"Dave! The dog—it's right there in the house. It's here, you know, like sitting around the corner here. Do you hear me? It's *here*!"

"Listen! Get a grip! First, take a deep breath. Relax and breathe."

The panic was welling up inside me until I thought I would explode. I said, "Yeah, it's easy for you to say, Dave."

"Listen to me a second, Robbie. Has the dog come into the main part of the house?"

"No. It's just sitting there in the Florida room panting, staring at us, and dealing stud poker. I think if it could, it would be tearing and rending the flesh from our bones. I need a little guidance and direction. What do I do here? Freaking out right now."

"Again, take a deep breath. Some of the protections are working, at least to the point where it can't come in, but there's not enough energy in those wards to repel it. Remember that corn I gave you when we were talking in front of my place to Carol? You still have it, don't you? Listen closely to me: That corn is no ordinary corn. It is sacred corn; it is very special. You need to count out 13 kernels right now and put them in your left palm. Close your hand around the corn. Fill that hand with white light. Imagine that the light of the sun is in the palm of your hand filling every one of those kernels. It's a bright, silvery-white light that is so bright you can see rays of it escaping between your fingers. Take three deep breaths. With each exhale, pack the kernels more and more with the white light you are creating. When you believe that you have infused enough power into them, just haul off and throw the kernels at the dog. Give it your most impeccable war cry when you hurl them. I'll leave work. I'll be there as fast as I can."

The phone clicked, then buzzed dead, leaving Penelope and me alone with the apparition. Sure thing, Dave, only hurry every chance that you get! I let the phone drop.

I ran to the bedroom to dig out the bag of corn from the pile of inconsequential objects on my nightstand. Fumbling and shaking like Don Knotts, I opened it up so I could pour the contents on the bed. I counted out 13 of the plumpest, juiciest, best kernels. The best-looking ones must be the most potent, but then, really, I was no expert on corn magic. In fact, what did I know? Nothing. So I grasped the kernels tightly in my hand. I could feel the little points at the ends digging into my palm. I tried to remember everything that any martial arts teacher had ever taught me about moving chi. I recalled every book I had read on psychic self-defense and on magic. In my mind's eye, my hand was glowing brighter than any supernova. You couldn't see my hand through the starlight that was radiating out. So this is what it was like to generate light, I thought.

I made my way back to the living room. Penelope, of course, was still sitting there in the gathering chaos, horrified.

"I swear, Robbie. This is the center of it all. This is the big evil eye from Hell. When I fall asleep, that's the bastard that rips me out of my body. I've never seen it look like that before. Why is it a dog?"

"I don't know. I've only seen the dog."

"It's daylight. How can it be here? What are we going to do?"

"Hold on. God I hope this works!"

I took a few steps forward. I could feel the thing daring me to come get it. But it didn't move. No easing forward, not a flinch, not a blink. It just sat there, staring at me with those pitch-black cavities, panting. The air grew thicker; the menace was palpable. I stopped in my tracks and closed my eyes. I saw the light in the corn. I could feel the weight of the light in the corn. I could feel the cold, white, burning light that was emanating from my hand. I *knew* it was good.

When I opened my eyes I couldn't see any of that comforting light. All I could see was the scary dog in front of me. I threw with all my strength and intent. I might have even yelled, "Get out!" I don't quite know for certain. I was sure thinking it very loudly.

I do know I heard a deafening cry in my head followed by a loud yelping of pain as the dog jumped back, and then turned and ran out *through* one of the walls. The baying started deep in my head, ripping its way out, tearing my brain matter to shreds on the way through my skull. I'm surprised I didn't wet myself. I was probably too scared. I looked over at Penelope, who was pale and shaking like a leaf in a thunderstorm. I'm sure if I could have seen myself, I would have looked the same.

She broke the silence. "Let's go outside for a minute. Please come with me, Robbie. I don't want to go out there alone."

When we walked out into the glorious Florida afternoon, Dave's black van came roaring up in to the driveway, him clinging for life to the steering wheel as it careened into the yard, digging ruts as he brought it to an abrupt halt. He jumped out of the front seat with a big grin on his face. "Is it gone?"

"The corn seemed to hurt it. Then it ran! That was some scary stuff, Dave. You have got to tell me what I need to do to keep that demon spawn from coming back. I don't want to go through that again—nope, no sir, not fun. Not fun at all!"

"Relax, will you? You would think you encountered a demon or something." He chuckled as if his joke was funny. "What was left in the room after the dog ran out?"

"I don't know. We came right outside to get in the direct sunlight. We didn't stop to look."

Back in we went. The energy was still stirred up in the house; the resident spirits were very annoyed. They made it clear that they didn't like what had been in their house. Not that I liked it, either. I could certainly relate. You could feel the whirlwinds of energy whipping all around inside the house. When we entered the Florida room, it was still bright and sunny. It felt really cozy and warm in there. We went looking for the corn. There were only two kernels surviving from the 13 that I had hurled at the beast. They were all shriveled up, the life sucked out of them. We looked everywhere, conducting a very thorough search of the room and the area outside of the room for any sign of the corn. The two anemic kernels were all that was left. But there was something else: We did find all these little spots—drops of what may have been oil, or maybe a thick ectoplasm on the floor near where the dog had been sitting.

Dave looked at the kernels and said, “Umm, you know, you may want to burn those surviving nuggets. They may have some essence from the creature left inside them. Yes, that would be the first thing I would do. Then I would sit down and meditate on a big sphere of white light that surrounds and bathes your house.”

“What are you talking about?”

“Intent is what is important here. That is where the real power lies. Trust me: If you meditate on a ball of white light surrounding this place and you have pure intent, the dog won’t be able to get through it.”

Dave laughed, then added, “Unless of course you like to entertain visitors from Hades?”

Dave got serious. It was about time in my opinion. “From now on you have to keep a smudge stick handy, at all times—at home, and keep one on you as well. When you build the white bubble of protecting light, fill it with sage smoke. Fire that stick up and feel the smoke fill the sphere. That’ll repel negative energies and let positive things pass. Do it.”

“I think Leigh has sage in her studio.”

I happened to look out the window and I saw Leigh pull up in to the driveway. Her friend Ella was in the car with her. Was it for the schadenfreude? No, not really. I watched for validation from a third party. I knew Ella was psychic. She can see and talk with those that have passed.

Leigh jumped out of the car, so happy to be home. She walked up to the back door. Ella stepped out of the car and looked as if she were about to swoon. She rocked unsteadily. She had to grab the roof and door frame to stabilize herself, avoiding a fall. When she did start to move toward the house it was with trepidation. She looked very reluctant to head forward. She had been to our house before; she knew about the ghosts. They had previously never concerned her, but she was hesitant to approach this time. I could feel her anxiety. Leigh turned saying something to prod her along. It was then that she half-heartily waved and smiled. Leigh started up the steps; I opened the door and gave her a kiss. I watched Ella as she took one step up the stoop then started to quickly backpedal, putting her hands up to ward off what was no longer there.

"It's okay, Ella. Whatever it was, it's gone now."

She just looked at me in disbelief.

"No really! We chased the thing off; it's safe to come in. Honest!"

Leigh turned to me and asked, "What do you mean 'thing'? What have you been doing while I wasn't home?"

We slowly walked toward the living room. Ella kept glancing around like she was going to see something very frightening at any second. Hesitantly, Ella sat down in the middle of the couch. She seemed kind of distant, like she was only half there with us. She was feeling things the rest of us weren't.

I sat down next to Leigh and explained, "Clevis's little devil dog came by for a visit."

Dave snickered, "When I got here they were still quivering."

"Leigh, you really should have been here. It was a relaxing afternoon."

Ella spoke up, wide-eyed at the dangers she perceived: "It's not funny one bit! This is serious. Your ghosts here in the house are really mad! They're scared to death. I don't know what was here. I do know it was really bad; it even scared the dead people. Y'all need to be very careful—very careful indeed!"

Her eyes glazed over for a minute, then, as if receiving some cosmic signal, she spoke again, "Oh, hurry and get me a piece of paper and something to write with! Hurry. I need it now!"

She started to mumble under her breath; for the most part it was unintelligible, but every now and then "hurry, hurry" could be heard quite clearly. Leigh returned from her sojourn and handed Ella a pencil and a small pad of paper. Quickly she jotted down:

Sasquawaha
Daughter to the tree
Spread wide your arms
Taking me in

Protect, preserve and guide me.

Ella shook her head for a moment, and looked back at Leigh. "No. Fetch me a pen, please. I need something permanent that can't be erased, accidentally or otherwise."

Then she turned to Penelope and said, "This prayer is for you. When you are at home and the bad things come to bother you, just look at that big oak tree in your front yard. If you can't see the big oak, at least picture it in your mind. Then say this prayer and the spirit that inhabits that tree will drive the nasties away. You do have a big oak in your front yard, don't you?"

Penelope nodded her head. "I just moved in. There is one at the corner of the yard. The road bends at a right angle around it."

I piped up, just to add my two cents worth, "It's pretty rockin'. When you hug this tree, you can feel it hug you back."

Penelope suddenly seemed very uncomfortable. She stood up and said, "I think I have to leave. Your ghosts are really mad and for some reason they want to take it out on me!"

Once Penelope had left, Ella became visibly more relaxed. "I don't know what she's been messing with. Whatever was here, it was evil—really, really bad evil."

She looked up; she finally realized that we knew very well how powerful this negative entity was. "All right, Leigh. If you need a place to stay my house is yours. You know you'll be safe there."

"I'll think about it. There just seems like there is always something here watching me—something more than the normal ghosties."

"You have a very powerful protector. It's pretty big, too. You really don't have to worry about anything. I don't think anything will get passed that guardian of yours. Maybe you've been feeling the protector hovering over you."

She looked over at the area next to Leigh; I could see nothing there. She pointed to the empty space and said, "Hey! Think you could back off a little? You're making the girl nervous."

There was a moment of silence. "You'll be better now. It won't hover. But if things get to be too much to put up with, come over. You don't have to ask, honey. Ella *knows*."

Chapter 16

Return to Gwen's Place

David

Little by little, you must create a mysterious fog around yourself; you must erase everything around you until nothing can be taken for granted, until nothing is for sure any longer, nothing...is real. Your problem now is that you're too real. Your actions are too real; your moods are too real; your life is too real. Don't take things so much for granted. You have to begin to erase yourself. Begin with simple things, such as not revealing what you really do.

What's wrong with how you live your life now is that once people know you, you are an affair taken for granted and from that moment on you won't be able to break the ties of their thoughts. Their thoughts will enslave you. I personally like the ultimate freedom of being unknown. No one knows me with steadfast certainty, the way people know you, for instance. Because of that, I have the ability to totally confound their lives.

From now on, you must simply show people whatever you care to show them, but without ever telling them exactly how you've done it. You see, in the end we only have two alternatives; we either take everything for sure and real, or we don't. If we follow the first path, we end up bored to death with ourselves and with the world. In addition, we end up boring to death those whose lives we touch. But, if we follow the second path and erase our personal history, we create a fog around us, a very exciting and mysterious state in which nobody knows where the bunny will pop out—not even ourselves. There is great power in that. Trust me.

Robbie

For some reason, I was not quite all the way to the end of the peninsula out at Gwen's lake. The landing was still another 10 feet or so in front of me. I had been out there for a while, but exactly how long was uncertain. One of the first things I had learned in my experiences with Dave was that time moves so differently when you are in medicine time. Finally, the last glow of the dying sun had disappeared from the night sky. There was no moon—just the twinkling light of the stars. Even the normal iridescent glow of the thick marsh was subdued. It was dark. There I stood, with still another fruitless sunset, attempting to "stop the world"—and as usual, nothing happened.

It was time to go in. I thanked the spirits of the lake and got ready to turn, when I heard a loud snap off to my right. The drone of the insects and frogs immediately stopped. An unearthly quiet engulfed the lake. Then, again, to my right was a loud crash. My mind raced. What was it? It was big; I could tell that for certain. The crashing through the brush got louder. Looking around, I realized I had about 150 feet to go to get out of the marsh and back into the yard. The crashing was heading right toward me. Male gators can grow up to 11 or 12 feet long and weigh as much as 1,000 pounds. They're fast, too. If they get up on those little legs they can run a man down. They are large, hungry lizards with big teeth. It was Florida, it was a lake, and there *were* gators.

I froze; I knew that predatory instinct would cause the gator to chase down the prey if I went running away, screaming in fear. I also became keenly aware that it wasn't twigs snapping; it was branches. It was loud enough to be small trees. The more I listened, the closer it approached. How could I run in a pitch-black swamp with deep water on two sides? The sad realization was that I was trapped. There was an open lake in front of me and no place to go. All I could do was stand and wait motionless, hoping I wasn't going to be dinner. It was agonizing waiting for the behemoth to materialize from the impenetrable darkness.

The cacophony was surrounding me. I was panic-stricken. The supernatural stuff was easy to deal with. This was Mother Nature; she can be unforgiving. How big was the gator? Oh my god—what if it was a feral hog? I was really freaking out. At least if it was a hog, I could jump into the lake with the gators to get away from the pig.

The tension was too much to bear. I caught movement out of the corner of my eye and quickly glanced down. There was a small black shadow coming out of the brush. It was hopping. Hopping?

It was a tiny black rabbit. The bunny hopped right up in front of me. It sat up on its haunches and looked me in the eye. I could hear him laughing in my head. The bunny was smiling at me—a big cartoon smile—and laughing! But the smile wasn't in my head; it was plastered across his little face. All his teeth flashed white in the darkness. After sitting there looking up at me, obviously amused, for a minute or so, the little black rabbit dropped down to all fours. It nonchalantly loped off to the left without a sound. The choir of critters around me then announced their evening performance. Crickets and frogs all sang out. I tried to listen for the rabbit, but there wasn't a rattle or snap. The ambiance had changed. It was brighter—lighter. I couldn't believe how scared I had been. I had been terrified. And it was just a bloody bunny.

I got back to the yard; a couple of the dogs came running up wanting to see what was going on. We walked back up the slope to the house, picking up four-legged friends on the way. At the back door, I pushed my way through the pack and walked inside. It sounded like I let a herd of cattle into the house. I went into the dining room; Gwen and Dave were sitting at the table.

"Those are some funny bunnies you have out there by the lake."

Gwen snorted. "Bunnies?"

She and Dave had a hearty laugh.

Gwen looked me straight in the eye and said, "Robbie, we don't have any rabbits on the property."

Dave looked at me sagely, posing a question: "How many dogs went with you when you went out to the lake?"

I thought about it a second. "Six."

"How many went out to the end of the trail with you?"

"At least three. They left after a while but joined me when I came back to the trailhead. By the time I had returned to the house the rest of the pack had joined me."

"Think about it for a minute. Those dogs love to chase down rabbits—and eat them. Trust us: There are no rabbits on the property."

"I swear I saw one."

They both laughed while I told them about the rabbit and how scared I was.

Dave wiped a tear from his eye, gasping for breath from laughing. "So, did the bunny walk on water to get to you?"

"No—wait. I know—it swung from branch to branch," Gwen quipped between giggles. "Like a little cotton-tailed monkey."

Dave looked at me seriously. "You know, no sane rabbit would be swimming out there at gator dinner hour."

Gwen couldn't help adding, "Oh no, Dave. Get my gun. I've got a cwazy wabbit on my property."

They both burst into howls of laughter again. It took a few moments before lucid conversation was possible again.

"With all the dogs, there are definitely no nosey rabbits around here." Dave looked at me, grinning. "That, little buddy, was no ordinary rabbit. You had a classic totem encounter.

"There are four levels of totem encounters. The first is when you have an affinity for a specific creature. You desire to decorate your house with pictures of mice, for example. Mouse could be your totem. Another sign could be if you see animal tracks often, but don't see the animal. Or even if you tend to run into the same creature in your dreams, that's the subtle way of meeting a totem.

"The second way is when you see a creature in threes. This usually means you have acquired an animal totem. Now, it could be a group of three all at once, or you could also see the same specific animal in a dream three times or in the field on three different days. But you definitely see the animal.

"The third kind is apparent if the animal acts in a way that's totally inappropriate to the situation. In a dream the animal could talk to you. Or in life the bunny could walk on water, or crush trees and snap branches while it walked. The animal will show no signs of fear; on the contrary, it will act just the opposite.

"There's an ultimate encounter with a totem animal but we should probably save that for a different day.

"You need to pay attention to rabbits now. The next time you see rabbits look at them closely and remember their qualities, pay particular attention to their behavior. If they are acting strange, pay attention to what they are doing, as their actions are important. They're trying to tell you something. I'm not sure what the properties of rabbit are, but you need to add this to your research. Tonight proves rabbit has a sense of humor."

I did the research. Rabbits are considered tricksters but more gentle than coyote. More gentle, my eye.

Dave

Funny how things can seem like total chaos, then suddenly all fall into place. The world has its own plan and goes about it in its own mysterious way. I was sitting out in my yard on a fine Monday morning and thinking about taking a trip over to Cassadaga. I wasn't sure why I would be going there that day; I just knew I would. Some folks plan a trip to the spiritual camp near Deltona, which only has psychics, mediums, and spiritualists for inhabitants; I never did. I always went on impulse, or by need. At that moment Penelope drove up in her station wagon.

"Penelope? Have you talked to Henry lately?"

"You know, it's funny you should say that. I went by his house yesterday. I know he was there, but he wouldn't answer the door. I could hear the TV on inside, and I swear someone was walking around, but he wouldn't answer the door."

"I think Henry is done with trying to help us. He had an unnerving visit."

"From whom?"

"You."

"Me?"

"Well, something that looked like you. And when it was done with him, he was done with this."

"Oh." Penelope looked a little sad. "You mean the thing came and looked like me?"

"Something like that."

"Hey, guys. Whatcha doing?" Stephanie bounced up into the yard.

Looking at Stephanie, I saw it. I had seen a light twinkling here and there, but she had never struck me as someone with much power. Now, in the brilliant light of the morning, she was glowing bright. It was not who I would have thought was going to help us, but power was pointing her out to me. She was shining—a beacon on a dark night. An idea struck me between the eyes like a molten bullet.

"Going to Cassadaga. Wanna come along?"

The scent of patchouli and sandalwood filled the van as we took 441 South out of town heading for Cassadaga. It's a good day trip—about two hours to get there. Penelope and Stephanie took the opportunity to get to know each other. Once Penelope had mentioned a haunted house, Stephanie was enraptured. Penny filled Stephanie in on the fun at her house, judiciously leaving out the goriest bits. That was good; I didn't know if Stephanie was up to full disclosure quite yet. If we picked the right psychic, out of all of the ones that would be available, she'd get it, real quick.

It was a little disconcerting; the small shops that led up to the spiritual camp were all closed. These were the unsanctioned and unaffiliated. Maybe the members of the spiritual camp had put a stop to it. I figured I would spring for lunch at the Cassadaga Hotel, a creepy place that smelled like a funeral parlor, but where the food was great. It was also the only place to eat in town. Cassadaga looked deserted; normally the town was rife with college kids, the spiritual, or the just plain curious. But that day, there was no one. All the shops were empty—locked up tight. Even the hotel was closed. I didn't even know it closed, and there was not a soul on the street. It was quiet, like something was waiting to happen.

"Looks like we picked a bad day to visit."

"Nonsense, Stephanie. This is simply perfect. No lines and the psychic of our choice. Does anyone want a reading?"

Penelope piped in very quickly, "No, thank you. I got a reading at the psychic fair and look at what that stirred up."

"Stephanie?"

"Actually, I would like to get a reading. Let's walk around and see if we can find someone who is open."

I led the way down the narrow streets crowded with houses. We walked by Spirit Pond; every door had a "Closed" sign.

Stephanie was the first to speak: "This place is like a ghost town. I guess I wasn't meant to get a reading today."

"That may be a good thing." Penelope smirked.

"Oh, ye of little faith." I laughed at both of them. "Someone here was meant to get a reading, all right. There is one medium that is waiting for us. We just haven't looked in the right place."

We got back to the van; it was then I saw the woman sitting on her porch across the street.

"Are you folks looking for a reading?"

Penny and I walked across the street toward the woman's house. Stephanie, of course, ran.

The psychic looked at her. "Are you sure you want to run to this?"

She then turned to Penelope and me, speaking in a knowing manner: "I drew the short straw today. No one wanted to be here for your visit. The reading is for this young lady here. Y'all know what you need to do; you don't need me to tell you."

A washed-out Stephanie came off the porch with a very serious look on her face. I asked her how it went.

"I am to help you. I am part of the group. You lost someone, and I am to take their place."

"Stephanie, if I were you I would go back in there and ask for your money back. She didn't do you any favors on this. Trust me."

"I am starting to get it, Uncle Dave."

Chapter 17

The Concert

David

The problem here, Robbie, is that you take yourself way too seriously, and I mean serious as a heart attack. You are too important in your own mind. Your perception must change! In fact, you are so important that you feel justified to be annoyed with everything. You're so important that you can afford to leave if things don't go your way. Just pick up your marbles and go home! I suppose you think that shows you have character. In the course of your life you have never finished anything because of that sense of disproportionate importance that you attach to yourself.

This magnanimous self-importance is another thing that must be dropped, just like your personal history. The world around us is very mysterious; it doesn't yield its secrets easily. As long as you feel that you are the most important thing in the world you cannot really appreciate the world around you. You are like a horse with blinders on; all you see is yourself set apart from everything else. This is folly at the highest level. We are nothing but dust in the wind my friend. We are no better or worse than anyone else. What sets us apart is not our importance, but our unbending will. So get out from in front of the false mirror of self-importance!

Robbie

Light Up Orlando! It was a huge event, with multiple stages and a hundred thousand plus in attendance. I was thinking it should be fun. We were lighting the main stage at Church Street Station. The artist was Weird Al. The venue provided spotlight operators, and Weird Al had his own lighting director, so I was there for setup, strike, and viewing pleasure. It was a straightforward setup; we banged it out then kicked back to wait for nightfall and the show. When the t-shirt guy showed up, I recognized him. We had toured together. Samantha and I would be getting swag tonight. It was a good day.

With plenty of time to kill, I set out exploring. I found myself wandering around the shopping and nightlife district of Orlando. As the sun began to set, the crowds got noticeably bigger. I found that I was really in tune with the people around me. I began to feel more and more impressions from them. I would look at someone and I could tell if they were angry. Wow, that group was high and happy. It was cool, at first. I have always been fairly empathic. But this was a different experience altogether.

As the crowd grew ever larger, the emotions bombarded me. The stronger the feelings, the more impact they had. I felt the emotions to the point of experiencing them. My body felt like it was angry, sad, and ebullient, both separately but sometimes all at once. Whatever dominant energy was in the near vicinity would impact me the most. My head was reeling. The streets were closed; there were folks in the road, shoulder to shoulder. So many people—so many—so happy, but there were those few that weren't so happy—those that had anger, hate, or sorrow. I could feel the negativity crushing down on me.

Looking for a brief respite, I slipped into one of the shops. It was a Western wear and Old West artifacts store. The press of partiers wasn't so bad inside the confines of this haven. I figured it would probably be a store with sterile shelves filled with a bunch of stuff made in China. I would at least be able to get a break in there. Amazingly, as I looked around, I realized it wasn't junk. It was actually genuine authentic Wild West memorabilia. As I walked through the store I could feel myself being drawn to different display cases. Certain objects that looked ceremonial radiated residual energy that was like a kick in the gut. I'm not sure how theses artifacts were acquired, but some of them emanated anger and vengeance. Even in there, I felt the petty emotions of people pounding me. Now, compounded with objects that were alive and reaching out, it became too much to bear. I put my head down and walked out of the store. There was something in the store tugging at me to come back, but it didn't feel like an invitation; it felt more like a dare.

The crowd was even bigger. The energy was starting to condense around the stages. I became totally disoriented. The weight of all the emotions crushed down on me, assailing me from all directions. I quickly found Samantha. I told her I wasn't feeling well; I needed to lie down for a bit. I assured her I would be fine for strike after the show. I climbed into the truck. Back in the corner of the box, I covered myself with all of the packing blankets and jackets I could find. I made a cocoon to shield me from the emotions. I spent the whole show curled up in the fetal position trying to turn off the bombardment.

It was a relief when the PA quit rattling the sides of the truck. I could feel the crowd dissipate. You always feel the change in energy after the show, but this was different. I could feel each departing soul, like pulling the stones off of an avalanche victim. As each person walked away, my breathing eased; the burden of their anxieties melted away.

Finally, when I emerged from the protective cave of the truck only the work crew remained. I could still feel whatever it was at the store around the corner. It was a nagging dare to come back and play. I also noticed an occasional emotional feeling pushed up against my psyche, but after the earlier onslaught it was easy to manage the brooding weight.

The next day, I broke down finally buying the book *Psychic Self-Defense* by Dion Fortune. Dave and I had discussed much of the concepts within its pages, but as I read it I found that it really reinforced the technique of building the white bubble of protection around yourself, but more important, how to keep it in place. I needed the reinforcement. The night of the concert—where I went that night—was not a place I wanted to go to again. Ever.

Dave

"So, Stephanie, just exactly what do you have faith in?"

"I practice Wicca. I've read everything on witchcraft and the goddess. I've had some luck working with elemental magic, candle spells, that kind of thing."

"Uh huh. Well, tell me, witchy-poo: Did you learn anything about demons in your studies?"

"There aren't such things as demons. That is just a Christian construct to villainize nature spirits."

"Really? Really?"

"Yes. Angels, demons—the Catholic Church put their own terms on things they needed to explain. Before that it was goddess and god and spirits. Why?"

"Because we are dealing with a demon here. It's more than a Bible belief. Every religious and spiritual tradition talks about demons. The Buddhists talk about how the demons are personality traits and foibles. Yet they depict them carrying swords and severed heads. I just don't see your anger or envy cutting off people's heads. The Indians have Ida and Kalona Ayeliski. Every pantheon, every tradition—there has to be a kernel of truth, don't you think? Demons are insidious and I wouldn't want you to get hurt."

"Yeah, Penny was telling me that, but I don't believe it's a demon. A really angry nature spirit—that I could believe."

"That will change. Ever go out to the Devil's Millhopper?"

"Oh yes. It's a great place of power."

"Ever go out to Payne's Prairie?"

"Sure. I drive past it every time I take 441."

"No, Stephanie. Have you ever actually gone out on the prairie?"

"Well, no. Not really."

"Then we shall have to remedy that."

Stephanie pleasantly surprised me on our trip out to the prairie. She manipulated the wind. She also worked her way around enough to find earth energy and play with it. She excelled at forming calm pools in the small creeks that run to the sink. It was a game to her. That would soon change.

"Why are you giving me all these tests, Dave? Don't you believe me?"

"It isn't a matter of belief, Stephanie. It's a matter of survival. When we go into battle mode everyone has got to pull their own weight. If there is a weakness among us, it will be exploited, and someone will get hurt. Robbie and I can protect you, but we will also be protecting ourselves. So it's important for me to understand the limitations of your abilities."

"You don't believe me."

"No. Let's just say I will feel better seeing how you handle yourself in a variety of situations."

"You have to trust me."

"Stephanie, I don't trust myself. It is not a matter of trust. It is a matter of survival, plain and simple. If you have a weakness, I need to identify it, then try to address it before we have our backs to the wall. Any chink in your armor—this demon will find it and expose it for everyone to be aware of. If you have secrets or skeletons in your closet you need to come to terms with them. Those things and more will be used against you. In the days ahead, there will be attacks against us, probing forays that will test our mettle. I will find out what I need to know based on the outcomes of those attacks and how everyone reacts to them."

"You are taking this really serious, Dave. I don't think I have ever seen you like this."

"I always take life-or-death situations serious. Besides, you have never seen me deal with a demon before."

"How many times have you dealt with something like this?"

"Never."

"Oh..."

"Exactly."

Chapter 18
Stephanie and the Shotgun House

David

When a man decides to do something, he must act, and in acting, he must go all the way. But he must also take responsibility for what he does. And no matter what he does, he must know first why he is doing it. Then he must proceed with his actions without having any doubts or remorse about them.

Look at me; I have no doubts or remorse. Everything I do is my decision and my responsibility. The simplest thing I do—take you for a walk in the woods, for instance—may very well mean my death. I am okay with the fact that death is stalking me. But because I am being stalked, I have no room for doubts or remorse. If I have to die as a result of taking you for a walk, then I must die. So be it.

You, on the other hand, feel that you are immortal. The decisions of an immortal man can be cancelled or regretted or doubted. In a world where death is the hunter, my friend, there is no time for regrets or doubts. There is only time for decisions.

When you get angry you always feel righteous. You have been complaining all your life because you don't assume responsibility for your decisions. To assume the responsibility of one's decisions means that one is ready to die for them. It doesn't matter what the decision is. It could be whether to buy green Gatorade or red; nothing could be more or less serious than anything else. In a world where death is the hunter there are no small or big decisions. There are only decisions that we make in the face of our inevitable demise. As such, they are all vitally important.

Dave

I woke up to a knock on the door. I checked my new alarm clock; it was 10 a.m. I stumbled out of bed and opened the door. There was Stephanie.

"Good morning, Uncle Dave. I've been thinking about what you said. Maybe my mind was too closed. I think you're right. We need to see if I have any weaknesses. So, is there some spooky place we can go and see what we can find out?"

"Would you like to go to the shotgun house?"

"The what?"

"The shotgun house."

"Why do you call it that? That's a weird name for a house!"

"Because a fella killed himself with a shotgun there a few years back. Wanna go?"

Robbie

Dave pulled up. Stephanie was in the van with him.

"Hey. We're going over to the shotgun house. You wanna tag along?"

I jumped in so we could drive down around the corner. We entered the weird little bubble of separateness that had come to envelop that part of the street since this whole ordeal began. Everything was muffled; there was a damper on all the outside sounds. Nothing could get in. It was one of the things that stood out, to the point of being deafening if you listened. If you weren't paying attention, you would probably never notice. I did; I noticed things like that. At least now I did.

Stephanie surprised me. She sensed immediately that things there were different, commenting when we got to the corner. Dave remained silent. We parked by the driveway and walked around to the front. Dave led Stephanie through the front yard. I knew exactly where he was guiding her.

Sure enough, she stopped dead at the suicide spot and said, "It doesn't feel right here. Something happened."

There wasn't a sudden noise or anything like that. Rather, it was more of an intuition that made us all turn in sync and look at the front porch. The curtain that was hanging in the left window dropped down as the hand pulled back. There was a gasp from Stephanie. We were being watched!

"I saw that," I told her.

"I did, too. Come on," Dave said, as he vaulted the three stairs toward the window. We all gathered around on the front porch, peering in. Nothing. We didn't hear anyone moving inside. We hadn't heard anyone scurrying from the window. Silence.

"I saw a hand holding back the curtain. When I gasped it let the curtain go." Stephanie was a little shaken.

"It doesn't look like anything has moved in there in years," I said as I gawked in through the dirt.

"We should go in and check," Dave piped up. "Try the door."

I reached over and turned the handle—locked tight.

We slowly walked around the house to the back door. A small set of decrepit stairs led to the cramped back porch—not really a porch, more a place to keep the washer that had a roof over it. Mudroom would be a more appropriate name. There was still an old washer and dryer sitting there rusting away, neglected. A patina of dust was everywhere. The ever-present spiderwebs were thick as bed sheets.

Dave motioned for Stephanie to lead us up the stairs. It was tight for the three of us; however, we all managed to fit. We tried to look in but could see nothing through the pulled shade. Stephanie reached out and turned the door handle. There was a loud click. The handle turned. She pushed lightly on the door; it didn't budge. She pushed a little harder. The hinges groaned like an eldritch screaming banshee. The space between the door and the threshold crackled and snapped as all the buildup of the years broke the bonds of reality. The opening widened slowly and painfully to about 6 inches.

Suddenly, Stephanie slammed the door. "I can't go in there, it's just not right."

"Nobody lives here. Let's investigate!" Dave whispered, demonstrating a firm grasp of the obvious.

"There is somebody there, Dave." Stephanie had grown a whiter shade of pale. "I am *not* going in."

She hurriedly pushed her way past us, heading toward the van at a crisp pace. I looked at Dave. He just grinned, shrugged his shoulders, and followed. I looked in the garage window as we passed. It was closed up tight; I couldn't see a thing. We piled into the van.

"I'm sorry. There was just something in that place that didn't want us there."

"You are afraid, Stephanie. You are really afraid of dying. You saw your life ebbing away as you opened that door, and you sensed your death stalking you. If you plan to take on what we are facing, there can be no room for fear, no room for doubt, no room for regret. There is only room for acts, and those acts must be deliberate, impeccable acts made with no hesitation, no fear. If you get scared when we face what lies before us, you will be destroyed, because neither Robbie nor I will be able to save you. You will simply be consumed."

"I was scared, Dave. It rocked me to the core. What I sensed was bad—very bad."

"And yet it was nothing compared to what we are facing. You are going to have to come to grips with your fear, and defeat it. There are far worse fates than death. To be afraid is to cede to fear. A warrior never yields to anything!"

We didn't go straight home. We drove a little loop first. Dave kept the conversation trivial—distracting. I knew where we were heading.

"What the heck!" Stephanie's head snapped to the right as we came up to the corner.

"Where are we, Dave? I swear something just tried to touch me. I feel like I need to take a shower. I feel dirty." Dave and I both grinned as she continued, "Is that Clevis's? Oh my God. I've never felt anything like it. Please, let's move on, okay?"

Dave snickered, in a most evil manner, "It's really too bad we've worn out our welcome. You should feel what it's like on the land itself."

"How could Penelope live there?" Stephanie was amazed. "I think I would have trouble living on this block."

"Now see, herein lies the problem," Dave answered. "If you were to come here alone, I would be inclined to think you would feel a welcoming energy. You would feel comforted, like you were at home. Then slowly but surely the evil would work its way into your head until you were ensnared with no way out. It would then hang you up by that pretty long hair and suck that loving energy right out of you."

We drove back to my house while Stephanie tried to reconcile what was happening. When we got there Dave parked the van and we all went into the house.

"Stephanie, sit down. I'll get you a glass of tea."

Dave flopped down on the sofa, patting the area next to him, watching Stephanie, and said, "What's the matter? You should be okay now."

"I think something followed us. I can feel something off in the other rooms. How did it follow us here?"

I laughed. "There's no one here but us and my roommates."

"That's not true! There is something else here I can feel it!"

"Stephanie, darlin', two of my roommates are dead."

"What are you talking about?"

"My house is haunted, too."

"This is good!" Dave broke in, "What I think we need to work on today is discernment. When you learned your Wiccan ways did you by any chance have a teacher?"

"Well, no. I had some friends in high school. We explored together. Since I moved up to Gainesville I've kinda been trying to figure it out myself."

"Most of the literature discusses two kinds of hauntings. There is the residual haunting. These are energetic impressions that are replayed like a tape machine. People, like ourselves, who can perceive the frequency can experience the event over and over again. Then there is your dime store poltergeist, that's the one that moves stuff and makes all the noises. There are, however, many more fish in the sea. Take the two spirits in this house. Robbie can tell you they interact with people in a conscious fashion."

I nodded my head in agreement and said, "It's downright uncanny."

"They really can't hurt you," Dave continued, "and have no intention to. They are just two lost souls who don't want to leave what they are comfortable with. The shotgun house now is something else. It's haunted yet there is something more there."

Seizing the moment, I interjected, "There wasn't any problem really until we started dealing with Clevis's. The house was creepy but it didn't reach out and say hello like it does now."

Dave nodded. "No. There is an older presence there that is angry about being disturbed and is just lashing out. Then there is Clevis's. What did you think, Stephanie?"

"That property made me feel dirty; that's the only way to describe it. I felt violated when we drove by."

"Do you understand now? Why I wanted to see where you stood?"

"Yes, I do. But I think—I think I might have some work to do."

"Just reflect about the different encounters you had today. Remember what each feels like. Some you can ignore no problem. Others ignore at your own peril. But you need to discern which is which. There are a lot of different spirits out there, don't be fooled by semantics. What you call them doesn't change how they interact with you."

"Dave, that's not fair." I pointed out one fact that I felt was important: "You know every time we drive by that house something tries to reach out and slap us. Stephanie got to see the place in its aggressive mode."

"Again, just as it should be. Stephanie needs to see it at its worst so when she drives by later she will know what's under the façade. Unless it got her scent, then there is no telling..."

"Are you trying to scare me, Dave?"

"No, Stephanie. I'm being straight with you. You can back out now and walk away. It will be very dangerous if you continue with us."

"You, I, and the psychic know that's not going to happen. It's just fear. I'll deal with it."

"Hey, wait a second. If she gets a choice of walking away, don't I?"

"Robbie!" Dave started to laugh again. "What makes you think you ever had a choice of being involved in any of this or not?"

Chapter 19

Stephanie Goes to Gwen's Place

David

I'm guiding you. I am not being arrogant; I know what I'm talking about; someone taught me all this. I didn't figure it out for myself. I didn't read it in a book. I didn't watch it in a movie! I'm having a lesson with you. Other people have had a similar lesson with you; someday you yourself will have the same lesson with others. All through your life from this day forward, people will move in and out of your life, as you need them, simply to have a lesson with you. Let's just say that today it's my turn.

One day I found out that if I wanted to be a hunter worthy of self-respect I had to change my way of life. I mean a total reversal of my ways. I used to whine and complain a great deal. I had good reasons to feel the way I did. I am part Indian, and Indians are treated like dogs. When I was growing up, it wasn't cool to be an Indian. There was nothing I could do to remedy that, try as I might, so all I was left with was my sorrow. But then my good fortune spared me and someone taught me to hunt. I realized that the way I lived was not worth living—so I changed it. It was really that simple.

Leigh says I laugh too much. I laugh a great deal because I like to laugh; yet everything I say is deadly serious. And this is the most serious thing I can tell you at this very moment. During times of power, the world of ordinary affairs does not exist; nothing can be taken for granted. Never forget this—ever.

Robbie

The cards said it was okay to try the ceremony that day. Not really; it was very ambiguous. But the cards didn't spell out doom and gloom. Everything else seemed to point to a yes; all the alignments were in the right place. Dave decided that sunset would be the most advantageous time—the crack between the worlds and all. I picked up Stephanie at 4 p.m. The drive through the pine forests was refreshing.

Stephanie broke the serene silence. "Thanks for picking me up. I'm so glad we are going to finish this tonight. I have a friend who lives around the corner. She always thought there was something funny about her apartment. It's haunted, of course, but nothing major. Lately, though, it's really been getting bad. Cabinets won't stay shut. The lights are flashing on and off at all different times of the day and night. She keeps bugging me to come over and help her out. It's really become a huge distraction. I don't need both things going on at once."

"I know. The shotgun house reaches out and tags me every time I get anywhere near it. It's trying to convince me I should be paying attention to it. It's just distractions to keep us from the task at hand."

We were a pair. Stephanie had the Stevie Nicks earth momma vibe happening. I had a crystal dangling from the ear and a medicine bag hanging around my neck. In the back seat we had a couple of bags with candles, spring water, and, of course, the crystal. We were armed for bear—or demon, perhaps.

The road to Gwen's house felt welcoming as we turned from the hard top to dirt. The late afternoon light shone with a golden glow through the trees. The smell of green and dust was comforting as always. In short time we pulled up by the house. Dave's van was there. I pulled in behind him.

When we walked into the house the vibe was different. The energy was stronger, with a tense undercurrent. The dining room was cleared except for the table, which had several candles on it. There was a white circle on the floor around the table. The dogs were outside. They normally had run of the house.

Dave greeted Stephanie and me. Then he asked, "Hey, since you weren't so happy with your last reading why don't you throw the cards again? I think you should do it at least once more before we start."

"I don't know, Dave. Things seem cloudy." By and large, I have a close connection to my Tarot cards, so I was rather earnest when I spoke, "I'm not really feeling it. Even when I asked the cards for permission it was with a real spirit of 'ehhh.'"

I threw the cards. Mediocre.

"These cards aren't really all that positive, Dave. I have a tenuous 'yes' at best. It's a true milquetoast Tarot reading. Pretty similar to the one I had earlier. It's y'all's call."

"What do you think, Gwen? I think we can keep going."

Gwen nodded. "Everything I looked into said it was a portentous time to do it. I agree. Stephanie?"

Stephanie shook her head in the affirmative. She and Gwen proceeded to gather up things in the house that would be requisite for the banishing. Dave said we needed to do a perimeter walk before we started. The pack accompanied us on our stroll. We would stop, Dave would face off in the direction away from the house, and I would hear him mumbling. When we got to the walk that led off into the lake Dave stopped, saying I needed to do the next part by myself. I went down the path to where I could stand out on the platform. I could feel the lake rise and fall beneath me. I thanked the spirits for helping us, for watching over us. I asked them to give us strength in the hours to come.

Everything was brighter, more vibrant; the smells of the marsh filled my being. I fairly skipped down the walk back to where Dave was waiting. We continued our circuit. The frogs and bugs serenaded us as dusk approached. Now the places that had seemed too dark to peer into were lit. I could see every leaf; every lizard that scampered would flash before me. The swamp was alive. Even in the creeping long shadows, there was light in the forest. We finished the full circle and then headed back to the house.

When we walked in, Dave noticed Stephanie was missing. "Where's Stephanie? We can get started now."

"She's lying down," Gwen replied. "She's feeling pretty bad. It wasn't right; it came on very quick. She was fine then she could barely stand up."

I stepped out on to the back porch. It was dead quiet. The jingle of collars and occasional panting from the dogs were all there was to be heard. No frogs, no crickets—this wasn't right. I turned, heading back inside.

"I think she'll be okay. Something kicked her butt proper," Dave said. He had a serious look on his face. "She just needs to get a little sleep. How did something get through all the defenses you have up around here?"

"You tell me, Mr. Wizard. You helped with them. Clevis apparently has some strong allies. We would have been okay if we were in the circle. We just never made it in time."

With that, we all sat down in silence. About a half hour later, Stephanie came out of the back room looking washed out and shaky.

"I'm so sorry for getting sick. I screwed everything up."

"Don't worry. Everything has a reason," Gwen said, guiding her to a comfy chair. She put a throw over her shoulders. "It wasn't supposed to happen tonight."

The weakest link had taken a hit. Dave and I helped Gwen restore the room to normal. Once the circle around the table was swept up, the dogs were again given sovereignty of the house.

Before we left I threw one more Tarot. I felt much more connected, like a veil lifted. The cards indicated that night would not be a good night to proceed. It was time to go home and sleep on the whole thing. Stephanie let us know she felt okay; she was ready to head back into town. We grabbed our things; Gwen and Dave walked us out. The door opened to a dark silence. The lakes and swamps of Florida are far from quiet, especially that early. Dave looked at Gwen. She raised an eyebrow in response.

"You need to be very careful on your ride home," Dave said, with a look that was akin to ice. "Keep an eye on what's around you. Be aware! Call me as soon as you get home. Remember the white light."

"A little melodramatic, don't you think?"

"Shut up and just call. You two are in dire straits until you get back to Gainesville. There are things stalking both of you! Whatever you do, don't stop."

As Stephanie and I turned the corner of the house, we heard the front door close. It was a subdued night, quiet with nothing moving. The trees didn't even glow as much as they normally did. Still, deep down, I knew as long as I was down there by the lake I was okay. Dave had me worried about what waited at the end of the dirt road.

We slowly drove away; we didn't even have to yell at the dogs to go back home. The headlights cut through the dark underneath the canopy of oaks. The moss hanging down, throwing weird shadows, was the only thing spooky. We turned out on to the asphalt heading to Gainesville. Stephanie leaned her seat back and tried to nap. I was left in the dark with my thoughts.

What's worse: the abrupt scare that jumps out and grabs you, or the slow, dawning realization that you are truly screwed? What happens when the nice forest with the bunnies and deer has become the nightmare forest from *The Wizard of Oz* on the path beside you wanting to tear out your heart? Somehow it snuck up on us. We were not alone. Dave had been right.

The first clue was when the car stopped but the road with the world kept moving underneath it. The feeling of acceleration—forward momentum—and then reality just left us. I made furtive glimpses out the window; the shadow was like a creature from a grade B horror movie. The faint flashes and dark shape let me know in no uncertain terms that we were not alone. There was something outside the car, something evil. It was moving with us, trailing us—stalking us. The entity kept moving to evade the landscape as the brush shot past us. I surrounded the car with a ball of the brightest white light my mind could conceive. Hopefully the ball was sealed tight. We kept on locked in a dream perspective, the landscape moving but we were sitting still. But we weren't.

I realized it was not a something I saw outside the window; it was some things. Just glimpses now and again, but there were definitely *shadows* running along beside us. It did not feel like spirit guardians giving us an escort. This was not all love. I looked over at Stephanie. She was sitting straight up looking out the window.

"I hope you are seeing what I am."

"There are dogs running alongside the car. Why are we going so slow? Just drive past them, Robbie."

"We're doing 65."

"Then go faster!"

The things, now fairly corporeal, were on both sides of the car. And although, to Stephanie's credit, a few looked like dogs, some of the others—well, not so much. I don't think a two-legged dog could keep up with us, yet something definitely bipedal was. Whatever it was, I don't believe it was of this world. Under Stephanie's encouragement I pushed harder on the gas. The speedometer read 90 but it was like we were sitting still with the landscape flying past us. We were immersed in the malevolent pack—jaws snapping, bodies jumping, skipping, weaving in and out of the this world and the next...flying by us... blinking in and out of reality. Yet, they were also constantly coming back to glare in the windows, daring us to step out. Most disconcerting was how they had to avoid obstacles. Hallucinations would not have to avoid the real world spinning by, would they?

Maybe another vehicle coming down the road would break the spell. I scanned the darkness ahead, but no help was coming from that direction. That was the night everyone decided to stay at home. I know out here people go to bed with the sun, but there had to be someone else out. The speedometer was touching 100. I looked over at Stephanie. Her eyes were wide, not looking at the road screaming by but at the maniacal pack bounding all around us. I could see it now: "Why no, officer, you didn't see all the hellhounds that were after us?" Luckily the excuse wasn't needed. As we came up to the edge of the fairgrounds entering Gainesville, the creatures started to peel off, leaving just our familiar nemesis, the black-eyed Hell Hound. We got closer to the intersection of Waldo Road, the dog stared in, waves of evil pouring over us. It was pushing the game to the bitter end.

A jolt ripped through my body as my perspective flipped back to reality. We were flying toward the intersection at full speed. I heard a nasty, maniacal laughing in my head getting louder and louder. The light was red as we went screaming toward Waldo Road. Just as we reached the intersection, the light turned green. When we reached the other side of the road, everything went back to as normal as it ever gets. I lifted my foot off the gas; the car slowed down to the speed limit. I took a deep breath and tried to get my heart to quit racing.

"I'm glad you saw that." I looked over at Stephanie. "No one would ever believe me if I told them what just happened."

"I'm not glad I saw it," she whispered.

We somehow made it back to her house without incident. We were both pretty shaken. We didn't say a word for the rest of the ride.

When I got home I went in and called Dave. I said, "Well, we're home."

"When you left, all the frogs started singing again. So, was I being melodramatic?"

Chapter 20

The Floor That Wasn't There

David

The other day, when that demon dog let out a scream, you moved very well. Everything you did then was done within a proper mood. You were controlled and at the same time abandoned. You were not paralyzed with fear. Attacking it with the sacred corn as you did, with intent, required that you hold on to yourself and let go of yourself at the same time; that's what I call the mood of a warrior. I wanted to show you that you can spur yourself beyond your limits if you are in the proper mood. A warrior makes his own mood. You didn't know that. Fear got you into the mood of a warrior, but now that you know about it, anything can serve to get you into it.

Robbie

Hauntings are, I thought, confined to a place or a person. However, if a place is haunted, it can make it easier for other things to come by. It was that or I was just seeing things I had never noticed before.

The university auditorium always seemed more like a Gothic church than a performance space. In fact, when originally built, it was the college chapel. The inside has open dark timber beams that support the roof above it. The shorter beams had gargoyles that looked out over the audience. They weren't your normal gargoyles, though; this was collegiate gothic.

There were six groups of four. The first guy was a scholar wearing a mortarboard; he held a book open in front of him. There was the musician with the frou-frou hat holding a lyre. The engineer, stogie hanging from to corner of his mouth, with his bowler at a rakish tip, held a gear in his hands. And a football player, ball in hand, looked tough in his leather helmet.

It was during a setup; I was in the booth looking out at the stage on level with the gargoyles. Movement caught my eye. The scholar was looking at me. He had turned his head and was looking at me. It wasn't malevolent—just looking. Somebody yelled from the floor. I looked down to change the fader on the lighting console. When I looked up he was gazing out like normal. I tried to rationalize it as being my overactive imagination. I am sure of what I saw. But then, many things are not as they seem in the university auditorium.

Dave and I got into the elevator. We pressed the C button to head to the control room. It should be stated that, as the house technicians, you learn every nook and cranny of your facility. You just never know when you have to find some long lost prop or snake a cable to the stage to power some special effect. We knew that auditorium inside out. It held no secrets from us, except one.

Perhaps, if there had been an abrupt stop, a flicker of the lights—some indication that we were entering the Twilight Zone—it would have been easier to explain. But no, the elevator just stopped between the second floor and the control booth. We were talking—not paying attention. I can assure you that there is nothing between the second floor and the control room.

When the door slid open we knew it wasn't right. The first thing that struck us as odd was the fact that it was way too dark. The booth at least had emergency exit lights that never went off, plus the windows that looked out on the auditorium allowed ambient light from the brightly lit hall to bathe the room in a warm glow. The second floor had huge windows that let in the daylight; at night, the outside street lamps and walkway lighting lit up the space. This floor looked abandoned. A preternatural haze hung in the air. A chair was barely visible in the dark overturned against the wall. I stuck my head out and looked around. Was there something waiting for us out there in the gloom? I knew that room wasn't there.

I leaned back in and asked, "Are you gonna get out?"

He looked out of the door, then back at me. "No way! I didn't lose anything out there. Are you?"

"Oh, no!"

I started punching the door close button. I kept hitting it until the doors sealed. When we came to the control room, as the door opened I held my breath. It was, at least, the place I was familiar with.

The rest of the night was rather dull after that. By the time we had made it home our perspective had changed.

"I don't know, Dave. We should have gotten off."

"That's the hardest thing to know. Did we miss an opportunity?"

"But what was it?"

"Tool or trap—I just don't know. It was a surprise!"

Overhearing our lighthearted reflections, Leigh just laughed. "You two are just having a regret fest—a pity party."

"Well, we should have at least gotten out for a minute. Just not let the door close."

"Really? Would y'all really have gotten out of that elevator?"

"Oh no!"

Chapter 21

Matt and the Catwalk

David

Acts have power. Particularly when the person acting knows that those acts are his final battle. There is a strange, consuming happiness—a peace, if you will—in acting with the full knowledge that whatever one is doing may very well be one's last act on earth. Your acts cannot possibly have the flair—the power or the compelling force of the acts performed by a man who knows that he is fighting his final, ultimate battle. I would highly recommend at this time that you reconsider your life and bring your acts into that frame of reference. Your life certainly depends on it now. You simply don't have time, my friend. That is the misfortune of being human beings. None of us have sufficient time. We are all going to die. No one leaves here a winner. There is something out there waiting for me, for sure.

Use it. My death advises me. How? It tells me it hasn't touched me yet, so I continue on. Focus your attention on the link between you and your death, without remorse, sadness, or worry. Focus your attention on the fact you don't have time; let your acts flow accordingly. Let each of your acts be your final battle—your end game. Only under those conditions will your acts have their rightful power. Otherwise they will be, for as long as you live, the acts of a timid, insignificant man—a buffoon. There is no time for timidity, only time for action.

Robbie

I had to go up to the catwalks at the auditorium to check a lighting position for a front of house truss. Matt, one of the student crew, went with me. He hadn't been up there many times. He just wanted to get a climb in when there was no pressure to perform. We walked through backstage, then up to the organists' room, then out onto the organ loft. Attached to its back, behind the pipes, there was a wooden chicken ladder that led to a platform where you could access the organ pipes. From there you had to set up an 18-foot extension ladder that went to the catwalk. We climbed up and caught our breath. Getting up there was an ordeal in itself, not to mention the care we had to take climbing through the forest of delicate metal and wood columns. One false move and it could cost hundreds of thousands of dollars to repair.

The light in the overhead grid was provided by the row of lamps that lined the walk joined by the bright sunshine streaming up from the windows below. Matt walked with me out to the end of the catwalk. The main struts jutted out an additional 8 feet from the end of the ceiling clouds. I needed to see exactly how far out. I climbed over the handrail to walk out to the end of the beam. It was 70 feet from where I stood to the floor below. Cheerful thoughts raced through my mind.

As I looked down, the vision filled my head. In perfect Hollywood slow motion, I saw the breathtaking fall: the exaggerated swan dive off the edge of the grid, followed by the flawless single flip, culminating in the sickening, bone-crushing, crashing slam on the seating below. I could see myself laid out forming a perfect broken "T" on the seats beneath me. There I was, staring to the sky, smashed and bleeding. A hard shove between my shoulder blades broke the vision. I rolled my shoulders forward to dissipate the energy. Something had tried to forcibly push me off the I-beam—something that wasn't there!

I shook my head and turned to get back on the catwalk. I looked over at Matt. He looked very strange. Matt was a big boy, definitely big-boned—probably big enough to play college football should he have the notion to. He was a nice guy, too. He had a good heart—truly a gentle giant. Still, during his summers away from college, he earned a living as a bouncer in the country redneck bars around Ocoee. Not a person to trifle with.

Matt looked scared—petrified really. He was holding each side of the catwalk rails. I could see that his knuckles were white. He was shaking. "It went through me."

"What?"

"It went right through me," he quivered.

"It's okay, Matt. It's gone."

"But you don't understand. I felt it go right through me."

"No, no. It's okay. It's gone. It was after me, not you."

He looked at me, shaking, his face washed out. The statement gave him a much-needed pause in his panic.

He reluctantly released his death grip from the rail and followed me to the ladder. When we got to the landing, I turned to ask him how he was. I noticed that there were tears streaming down his face.

"I'm okay. Let's just get down."

We took a moment to seek composure.

"Matt, I'm sorry, man. That was meant for me. You just were in the wrong place at the wrong time. The moment's gone now; you have nothing to worry about. Climb on down. I'll steady the ladder from here. It's cool."

He slowly climbed down while I steadied the top. When he got to the platform behind the pipes he heavily sat down. I scampered down to join him. Matt was sitting there, his face in his hands. His body was heaving as he cried. I sat there as he let it all out. After about five minutes he wiped his eyes and said, "I'm okay. Let's get out of here."

We climbed down the second ladder; he collapsed again on the floor. He sat there, this huge big guy, tears streaming down his cheeks. When he seemed a little more together I went to get Dave.

"Where have you guys been? I thought you fell or something."

"Funny you should say that. We had a little visit in the catwalk. Whatever it was went through Matt. He's pretty shook up."

Matt was still sitting on the floor behind the pipe organ. He had his knees held tight against his chest. He was rocking slightly but was a little calmer. The occasional tear was still running down his face. We stood on each side of him and put our arms around him, leading him out of the building. We went to the loading dock where Dave's van was parked. He opened up the back doors to access the black footlocker that was stowed away in the rear. He flipped open the trunk. It was an armory of spiritual weapons. There were candles of many different colors, several knives, bundles of herbs, and all kinds of feathers. It was a familiar thing to me, Dave's magical box-o-goodies.

"Matt, look at me." Dave dug out a black candle and a white candle, and gave them to him. "Trust what I tell you to do, and do it exactly like I tell you to do it. Burn both of these together until they are nubs. That will banish any residual energy that might be left behind. Then burn this sage bundle. Light it up, and when the flame is out, let it smoke around your whole apartment. Make sure you get smoke into all the corners, upper and lower; pay particular attention to the doors and windows. This will drive away the darkness and bring a positive energy to your surroundings. Your body has had a shock, just like death. A body that isn't prepared for it does not leave unscathed."

We walked Matt to his car and saw him on his way.

I turned back to Dave, who was watching Matt's taillights fade away. "So Dave, is he going to be okay?"

"He'll be okay. How are you?"

"I'm fine. Why?

"That was something sent from Clevis's. I think the swan dive vision was meant to enthrall you. Suck you in to the point where the shove should have easily tumbled you."

"So it was trying to kill me?

"Maybe just bang you around a little bit. Lucky for you it didn't work. Unluckily for Matt, he came along for the ride. It can be tough when your view of reality is shattered by something as cold as death penetrating your body."

Chapter 22
The Graveyard Around the Corner

Black Eagle

Once you know what it is like to collapse the world you realize there is a purpose for it. You see, one of the ways of the warrior is to collapse the world for a specific reason and then restore it again in order to keep on living. Someday you will live like a warrior, in spite of yourself. I have taught you nearly everything a warrior needs to know in order to start off in the world, storing power by himself. It takes a lifelong struggle to be by oneself in the world of power. It is time for you to go, to be kicked from the Hawk's nest. I have done what I could do. The rest is up to you.

Robbie

My friend Samantha lived on a road that literally dead-ended. The backside of the Mt. Pleasant cemetery began just beyond where the pavement stopped. Some of the more prominent black ancestors of Gainesville are buried there, but not in the back half. The cemetery is a strange place even as graveyards go. The back is truly a jungle, but as wild as it is, the back is not the oldest part of the grounds. The oldest parts of the grounds are up at the front of the property by 13th Street. Everything in the front is nicely manicured and mowed.

The area in the back was different. There were recent graves there. It seems like someone would come in, hack out a space, dig a pit, deposit the body, and go, thank you very much. Even creepier was the area where they buried the indigent. Deep in the recess of this area the paupers' caskets had caved in, giving it the feel of a Hollywood zombie movie set. Add this to the scads of underbrush, and moss-laden trees and scrub, and the back area had a real spooky feel. In stark contrast, the front was truly a place of rest, always clean, neat, and peaceful. We started our expedition there.

"Have ever you wondered why you never see any kids in this graveyard?" Dave asked. He had us standing at the front gate.

I thought about it. "This is too peaceful and nice. They don't know about the spooky end. And, if they park at the back they have to deal with Butkus. He's scarier than any ghost."

"While that could be true," Dave said, chuckling, "they don't have to play 'beat the ogre.' There are other ways in. There's the old drive-in theater over there. Kids run amok in there all the time, particularly with their bikes and their skateboards—all the time. What a dare it would be, to leave from the closed down drive-in and sneak into the graveyard. And for the redneck kids, go knock down a tombstone in the black cemetery. It doesn't happen, though."

"I'm always comfortable when I cut through here."

"You like graveyards and you respect the space. You would get much more pleasure hiding behind a tomb and jumping out to scare a vandal than you would by actually vandalizing anything here. Don't think the residents don't know it. There is, however, one resident here who is the caretaker. He can marshal all the energy here and be quite formidable. Or she, perhaps. But the question is: who? That's the job for you! Go to it, grasshopper."

"What are you talking about?"

"Simple. All you have to do is find the caretaker. Tell me who it is."

We slowly ambled about looking at all the stones. I always loved graveyards. This one was no different. There were a few good epitaphs on the stones, but nothing to laugh over.

Toward the back there wasn't much to see. It was an overgrown mess. We had to duck the banana spiderwebs to get between spaces.

The palms mixed with the brush and ferns gave it a true jungle feel. Some graves back in here were only a couple of years old but completely overgrown—nearly hidden entirely. Memorials and plastic flowers faded by the sun were enveloped by the land. Those graves that were older were sunken deep or creepier still, collapsed in on themselves from the decay of the wooden coffins. In some of the old graves you could actually see the pine boxes visible through the dirt. This was where the truly poor, unloved, or just forgotten were buried.

We spiraled toward a raised double vault in the middle of the cemetery. Janie and Rev. P.A. Daniels had a very comfortable tomb that I sat down on top of like it was a bench. I have respect, but come on—they're dead people; what do they care? Silly me. It didn't take long before I eventually got the distinct impression I should not be sitting there. Something pinched me, and pinched me hard! I broke some kind of record jumping down.

"I don't know, Dave. The Rev here seems to be particular about who sits on his grave. Of course, I know people sitting on my grave would annoy me. It is the only place that really stands out. The energy is strong. Is the Rev our secret player?"

"Yep, I agree with you. But I think you made him mad. Let's go for now before he stands up and gives us a sermon."

At dusk, Dave got up, stretched his body, which was making cracking and popping sounds, and said, "Let's take a walk, Robbie."

Dave and I headed up the road toward the barricade at the end of the street and the graveyard that lay beyond it. "I don't think the Rev really cared for the energy that is surrounding us right now. Let's go back and see if he has had a change of heart. You might get a totally different experience in the dark."

"I don't know. He might still be mad that I sat on his tomb."

After we stood there talking, something became visible. Standing between us at the barricade on the other side was a tall, shadowy figure. Smokey and ethereal, it was difficult to truly see, except for one very noticeable thing.

We were leaning on the fence, but between us were the distinct shadows of the 8 fingers that were wrapped over the edge. More like talons than fingers if the truth be known—sharp, bony fingers.

"I'm pretty sure he isn't in the mood for entertainment tonight," I conjectured.

Slowly we turned away from the fence. I did muster the courage to take one last look over my shoulder. The Rev stayed there as we walked down the street, just making sure we took the subtle hint. It was not wasted on me.

Chapter 23

Another Cleaning

David

There are entities in the world that act upon people. They are here, all around us, at all times. In daylight, however, it is more difficult to perceive them, simply because the world is familiar to us and that which is familiar takes precedence. In the darkness, on the other hand, everything is equally strange. Very few things take precedence, so we are more susceptible to those entities at night.

There is only one way to learn. That way is to chuck all the nonsense and get down to business. To only talk about power is useless. If you really want to know what power is—if you want to test it—you must tackle everything by yourself. I can't do it for you; I can only take you to places and make you accessible to it. The road to knowledge and power is very difficult—very long. Little by little you are plugging up all your points of drainage. The beauty of it is you don't have to be deliberate about it, because power always finds a way.

Power is coming to you in spite of yourself. Take me as an example. I didn't know I was storing power when I first began to learn the ways of a warrior. Just like you, I thought I wasn't doing anything in particular, other than surviving. But that simply was not so. Power has the peculiarity of being unnoticeable when it is being stored.

Robbie

I was feeling a sense of urgency. We all sat around the dining table at Dave's house. He spoke to break the pregnant silence: "We need to take care of this. It's really taking its toll on Penelope and I know it's hard for the rest of us, too. Let's do it tonight. We'll see what the cards have to say, then get it done."

Dave sat across from me, Stephanie was to my left, and Gwen to my right. I shuffled the Tarot cards, then placed the pile in the middle of the table. We focused our palms at the deck.

In unison we posed our question: "Is tonight the night we should do the cleansing?"

I passed the deck to Dave. He cut it three times. He passed it back, and I cut it three times. I flipped the first card over.

I placed the "Devil" in the middle of the table. This is the heart of the matter. This is the environment we are working with—the overall situation.

The next card was the "Moon." I laid that crossways over the "Devil." Above that I laid the card "Justice." Below the "Devil" I flipped the "Fool," eliciting giggles around the table. This was followed by the "Hanged Man." I couldn't wait for the next card. It represents the energy of the future—what was coming into power right then.

I flipped over the "Tower," possibly the worst card in the deck, for, unlike the "Death" card, which is actually fairly good, the dreaded "Tower" card always spelled disaster.

All of a sudden everyone became more serious. The cross was complete; I started on the staff. The top card was the "Hermit"—interesting. The next card, "Death." What card could follow that? "The Wheel of Fortune."

There is a tradition in Tarot: If two-thirds of the cards are major arcana, the reading is being guided by a higher source. I had never seen anything like that before. The next card was the culmination of the reading. The answer, if you will—the outcome.

I flipped over the last card. We sat there in silence. We just stared at the picture of a man lying face down on a shore with 10 swords driven into his back.

Dave was the first to speak. "I'm guessing here that the answer to the question is no?"

In light of what lay before us we all did the most sensible thing: We laughed and laughed.

"Here. I want you to have this." Penelope handed Leigh a stone necklace. "I'm tired of it but it may do you some good. An old Indian gave it to me out of the blue. He said it was a Navajo or Hopi snake necklace. The shamans would pull it taut and then throw it to the ground. It would slither off and get the information that the shaman needed. They also wore them for protection. It doesn't seem to be doing me any good. I thought it could help you because I know what's going on frightens you."

I took the necklace from Leigh. It immediately wrapped itself around my wrist. It was beautiful. Highly polished spheres of stone, a green turquoise sat next to an agate and deep brick red jasper. A disk of hematite separated each group. I noticed it liked to be woven about the fingers, a small snake wrapping up the hand holding it.

When Penelope left I turned to Leigh and said, "Don't wear that until I've had a chance to clean it."

"Don't worry. I wasn't going to!"

I looked up at the sky to the gathering clouds off in the distance. The air was still. The faint yet crisp smell of rain was in the air. The clouds were billowing up in all directions, except where we were. There, the sun was still brightly shining.

There were going to be some good storms. I decided go ahead and clean the necklace Penny gave Leigh. I took the necklace and put it into the ceramic goblet. I filled it with Rum Island spring water then walked out to the front steps. I set the goblet down on the brick wall next to the stairs. It was still clear blue above, but the thunderheads were starting to fill the whole sky. Occasionally a faint rumble could be heard in the distance.

"Spirits of the winds and the storm, please help clean this necklace of any negative energy that resides within it. Spirits of the water, please help remove the negativity of the necklace and restore it to a positive vibration." With that I went inside and sat down to talk with Dave.

The first warning breeze blew the trees outside. That's usually about a 10-minute warning. The five-minute warning *wind* blew through the open windows, bringing the cool comforting smell of the approaching moisture inside. Lightning started to flash more frequently; the time before the thunder sounded was shrinking fast. The first wave of rain came in heavy, pushed by a strong gust of wind. Massive explosions were sounding all around us as the lightning struck the grounds of the house.

We ran around the house like mad men closing every open window and door. As soon as the rain let up we could open everything back up. I got to the last open window and slammed it shut.

My ears popped! We desperately threw the windows back open.

The roar had come up quick hidden by the cracks and booms of the thunderstorm. Now, it was loud, unmistakable, the infamous freight train bearing down on the unsuspecting.

"The horror—just peachy." Dave held a hand to his head in mock disdain. "We're surviving fighting a demon only to be killed by a tornado. Oh, the irony! The horror *and* the irony."

I rolled my eyes at him as the wind screamed through the trees. The deluge of water pelted the house in loud waves. I threw open the front door and looked out. Past the screen door I could see nothing but an impenetrable white wall of water and wind, screaming louder than a thousand banshees.

Then, as fast as it came, it was gone. It was suddenly just our normal afternoon thunder boomers, with a gentle rain cooling things off very nicely. There was no indication that an F-4 tornado had just passed through the yard—that is, until we went out the back door to look around. At final count seven trees were down in our yard. The neighbors on each side seemed okay, but there were a lot of branches scattered on the ground everywhere. We walked a little down the street; in another yard the trees had uprooted and snapped like twigs. We went back, jumped into Dave's van, and headed east on 6th Street. All the way to 39th Avenue we followed the destruction. The tornado had hopped, skipped, and jumped through town; everywhere it touched down there was damage and destruction. The last place impacted was the Airport Lounge. The small, octagon-shaped building was hit pretty hard, the sign out front demolished, and the parking lot a study in chaos.

When we got back to the house I went out front to try to find the remains of the goblet. I was hoping to be able to find the necklace but

I wasn't counting on it. I mean, after all, a tornado had ripped through the yard, creating havoc. I walked out front looking down at where it had once been, expecting to see nothing.

It was sitting right where I had placed it. It was inconceivable. The necklace felt much better. It was glowing.

That evening, the weather service and TV news played down the whole episode, saying it was just a microburst of wind. I didn't know microbursts could skip like that.

"Robbie, do we still have water left?" Stephanie inquired. "There is an old friend of the family in town. He's really interested in the springs around here. I told him what's been going on. He found the spring water very fascinating."

"And you're telling me this because?"

"Look, he's a priest. Whenever he is discussing his job with my parents, they immediately stop talking when I come into earshot. He never really had a diocese. He was lucky; he gets to travel all over the world.

"He said he would bless some of the water for us. I don't know that I buy into his beliefs, but if we can get holy water I can't see where it will hurt."

"Catholic Priest?"

"Yes."

"For all you can say about the Catholic Church—you know, the Inquisition and such—they have been successfully fighting demons for a few hundred years or so. I think it will just make the spring water stronger. Every bit will help. I'll talk to Dave and give you as much as I can. Make sure you hit Dave up for some cash to put in the collection box."

"I'm glad you guys are together. You'll never believe what happened." Stephanie was all a twitter. "We have some great water now! I would have never known; it was amazing. I took the water to my friend. We went to the local church; I guess he had already made arrangements. We walked in; there was no one there. We went up to the altar and off to an anteroom to the side. I guess it was the local priests' private little shrine—a kind of special room, where they bless things?

"Well, on the ride over Father Benedict told me he had experience with the situations we were dealing with. They do not condone laypeople performing exorcisms but he knew me well enough to know I was following through with our ceremony. He told me that part of the blessing ritual involved adding salt to the water. He had salt distilled from the Dead Sea; according to him, the salt was especially powerful, having come from the holy land.

"When we got there he had me sit in a chair and get comfortable. He put on his vestments and opened a big Bible—well at least it looked like a Bible. All trimmed in gold. It had different passages marked out. He pulled out a purple bag and brought out a jar of salt. He poured a handful on the altar before him. He started to pray out loud in Latin. The only thing I understood was the occasional "In Nomine Patris, et Filii, et Spiritus Sancti, Amen." I knew that part so I always said amen.

"As he was praying the room kept getting brighter and brighter. There was something there; it was powerful. He pushed the salt up to the top of the altar, then pulled out the bottle full of the spring water. He poured it into a big silver bowl. He started with the prayers in Latin again. I'd never been moved by anything in Christianity like that before. The whole room was glowing bright—a powerful white light. The more he prayed, the more the room was filled with an incredible spirit of love. It flowed through us and around us. Father Benedict concentrated intently on the water in front of him. He sprinkled the salt into the water. The energy hit a crescendo, slowly coalesced, and poured into the bowl, lighting his face with love and spirit.

"When he was done he dipped his fingers in the water and did the sign of the cross. Then he dipped his thumb in the bowl and he reached over, placing his thumb on my third eye. Love exploded through my whole being. He did the sign of the cross in front of me. He then said a prayer for me and sprinkled the holy water in my face three times. He looked at me very intently and told me my fight wasn't destined to be his. However, if we got into real bad straits, he would help us.

"He said the living water from the spring was amazing. He could feel the power of the Holy Ghost surging through it. I get goose bumps just thinking about it. We have a nice sized bottle now; we should be able to really throw up our protections."

"Job well done," Dave tittered. "I love the irony of the church helping the witch get rid of the Evil. Maybe there is justice in the world."

Chapter 24

The Final Attack

David

There is something you ought to be aware of by now. I call it the sliver of chance. All of us, whether or not we are warriors, have a sliver of chance that pops out in front of our eyes from time to time. The difference between an average man and a warrior is that the warrior is aware of this.

One of his tasks is to be alert, deliberately waiting, so that when his sliver pops out he has the necessary speed—the prowess—to pluck it from the air and make it his own. Chance, good luck, personal power, or whatever you want to call it, is a curious state of affairs. It is like a very small string that appears in front of us and invites us to pluck it. Usually we are too busy, or too preoccupied, or just too stupid and lazy to realize that that is our sliver of luck.

A warrior, on the other hand, is always alert and tight, and has the spring—the gumption—necessary to grab it. Never forget this. The difference between victory and defeat is determined oft times by that tiny, seemingly insignificant sliver.

Robbie

The cards had at last foretold that it was the night. This night should be the night; ironically, it was Halloween. And a bright night it was, still close enough after the full moon that there was a round glowing disc in the October sky, bathing the landscape in an eerie blue light.

When I got to Dave's, Stephanie had already arrived. They had just finished clearing the living room of his apartment. The floor was empty.

"Where's Gwen?"

"She stayed at her house so she could better tap into her power. She's going to start at the same time we do."

Because Stephanie was our water sign she started by sprinkling our special blessed spring water in a large circle.

"I was going to make some sacred water of my own to add to the holy water. I started to research and found the pagan way to make holy water is the same as the Catholic—just different prayers. I don't speak Latin, so it could be the same prayers. I don't know." She encircled the whole living room.

Dave followed with a circle of sea salt. In the center of the room, he then drew another circle with salt that was 3 feet across. He then cut two lines across the center, making four quadrants that opened to the four directions. I removed the crystal from its blue pouch, took off the bindings, and placed it in the center of the circle, where Dave's X marked the spot. He had placed a broken shard of mirror there and had set several stones in a circle around it. The mirror shard had come from the shotgun house. He had retrieved it from an area near its mailbox, where an entire mirror lay in slivers and pieces. He had selected the largest piece the day before, noting how appropriate it would be for our purposes. It made a perfect reflector for the crystal and the stones arrayed around it. Finally, he placed a large violet candle next to the crystal.

Dave then turned off most of the lights, leaving only a few recessed sources in the rear of the duplex; it was pretty dim where we were. He put a boom box on the side of the circle closest to the front door. He handed me a tape. "Just turn it over when the first side is finished. We'll keep turning it until we're done."

The tape started; I recognized it immediately. It was the "13th Hour Chant" by Redbone, but only the first two minutes. I had been told it was a ghost dance chant to call on your ancestors. It definitely set an atmosphere, a trance-inducing combination of drumming and Native American chanting. And the bells—the jingling bells. Bells tied to the ankles of ecstatic dancers.

I sat to the East by the front door; Dave sat next to me to the South. Stephanie sat across from me in the West, and the space to the North was empty. We pulled out all our ephemera and power objects. Dave had six candles sitting in front of him, a pipe, a stylized knife, a ritual rattle, a wand, a medicine bag, and a selection of gemstones. Stephanie had half a dozen crystals, mostly amethyst, and a bowl of the holy water. I had a smudge bundle with a big feather, among the things in my quadrant.

Dave stood up, lighting a small bee's wax taper. While he was doing this, he thanked the spirits of fire for helping us. He picked up the red candle, lit it, and cried out, "Elements of Fire, guard us in the South!"

He walked behind Stephanie. She turned and handed him the blue candle. As the wick sparked up he said, "Spirits of the flame, guard us in the West!"

He walked to the empty quadrant. Stephanie handed him the green candle. "Elements of Fire, guard us in the North!"

When he got behind me I passed him the gold candle. "Spirits of the flame, guard us in the East!"

He moved back to his place in the South, picking up the white candle. "Nothing from above can harm us!"

He lit the last candle, "Nothing from below can harm us!"

He sat down; Stephanie stood. She followed the circle around sprinkling a blessing at each of the four directions.

"Spirits of the Rivers and Lakes,

Spirits of the Oceans and Seas,

Spirits of the Springs that bring forth the life giving waters,

All the spirits of Water, in all directions, in all forms,

Heed my call.

We honor and revere you.

We ask the Spirits of the water to protect us from all things negative,

Banish evil,

Allow only the positive to enter this space.

So Mote It Be!"

She sat down, taking a sip from the bowl of holy water. She then passed me the bowl; I did the same. Peace and love flowed with the water; they exploded through my body. I passed the bowl on to Dave. Stephanie finally took it back and placed it in front of her.

I stood up with the bundle of white sage, putting flame to it. I turned and faced the North; I blew over the top of the smudge stick and said, "Winds of the North, winds of winter, help us with our fight!"

I stood for a minute waiting until I could feel the slight breeze against my face. I turned to the East. "Winds of the East, winds of the sunrise and spring, help us with our fight!"

To the South I said, "Winds of the South, winds of summer, help us with our fight!"

And finally: "Winds of the West, winds of the sunset and autumn, help us with our fight!"

The winds howled outside the edges of the circle. Compounding the sound of the wind were the bells, drums, and voices chanting. There were more and more voices chanting in a cacophony of sounds that could crumble stonewalls. The ground shook; the walls trembled; the duplex seemed to hold its breath to keep from exploding with the power that was flowing up through us.

Underneath it all, I felt, more than heard, a buzz. Like a thousand angry yellow jackets, far, far away in the distance but moving ever closer. The angry buzz and howling of the winds lessened when I had to flip the tape. I thought when the tape ended it would have really put a damper on the flow. It didn't. It brought a snap of clarity in the middle of the storm.

Every time I turned I felt the tugging and pulling of countless little hands. Things were trying to pull me away from the strength of the circle. But when I turned back to the crystal and candles, I once again became one with the moment. The grasping became desperate; soon it was no longer a struggle to fend it off. It was growing weak. But then, so were we. We were pouring out everything we had in us, combining it with everything from outside of us, focusing it on one intense purpose.

Dave lit the violet candle. We concentrated on filling the crystal with as much white light as possible. We sat there; the buzz grew louder. The flames on the candles burned higher, the crystal started to really glow. It always had an inner light but at that time it was blazing. The room was vividly bright. Light began swarming in from all directions—a giant kaleidoscope spinning drunkenly out of control.

The echoes of screams underscored the buzz. The sounds were battering the outside of the house, just at the edge of our cocoon of Fire, Earth, Water, and Air. Around us, a thousand warriors from a time long gone danced, adding their bells, drums, and rattles to the din. The whole world held its breath.

Dave started the prayer:

> *"We allow only the best and highest to come through.*
>
> *The white light protects us.*
>
> *The violet light transmutes all negative energy into positive life force!*
>
> *And we send it back to the cosmos with Love."*

Stephanie and I picked up the cadence, joining in. With the tape going it felt like a chorus was praying with us. Outside you could hear the maelstrom howling in protest. Hundreds of souls all shrieking in their wretchedness and horror. As we continued, our visualization focused on Clevis's property. Every bit of space on his property was being inundated with waves of white light followed by violet tsunamis crashing down, flooding every inch. We kept the prayer up, over and over. Time ceased to flow.

The only thing keeping check on us, keeping us from completely disappearing into the energy, was the mundane act of flipping that tape. In the spaces you could still hear the spirits dancing and the demons howling in protest. At one point, you could almost see the shadow warriors spearing the minions around us. Eventually, the chanting continued even while the tape was being flipped and couldn't possibly have been playing.

Then, a super-nova—a huge, deep purple beam of light burst forth from the crystal, lighting the room, our faces, and the shadowy figures dancing around us in a beautiful, brilliant violet glow as it rocketed through the ceiling toward the direction of Clevis's house.

A vision burst forth in my mind: Clevis's property—the windows of all the buildings blown open by an emerald green light that slowly turned violet then white. I saw the waves of white and violet emanating from our circle into the crystal, blowing out through the roof in a beauteous purple beam. The light was pulsing over the property, a spectral rat catcher, seeking every shadowy corner and hidden recess in which vermin dwell. The hideous green retreated, inches at a time, then by the foot. Finally there was no more green, just a deep ultraviolet with beautiful white sparkles—snowflakes of light, falling on the land dissolving negativity into space.

We stopped the prayer, continuing to concentrate on the tableau in front of us, each of us sharing the same vision. When the green had finally disappeared, the annoying buzzing drone faded away as well. After a lifetime, the howl of the wind started to lessen, and then became inaudible, but we could still feel the occasional flirt of breeze touching our face and hair.

There came a definite change in the atmosphere. The unbearable weight we had struggled to carry for so long was lifted. It was done; the unseen foes were gone and the unseen allies that had come to aid us slowly started to leave, blending back into the shadows from whence they came. Dave thanked the spirits of the elements and extinguished the wick in front of him with his fingers. Stephanie and I followed suit. I put out the candle in the North before mine. Dave put out the black and white candles, leaving just the violet candle burning next to crystal. We sat for a bit longer in the glow of the aftermath, catching our breath.

Dave finally reached over, putting the flame out on the violet candle and saying, "It is done."

In his wonderful, subtle way he got up and turned on the bright overhead light in one of the other rooms.

"Ah man. That's cruel." I was waking up from a dream. I had just returned from another place—a darker place; everything was brighter. When I stepped outside I could see the life in everything around me; the trees glowed. The night was calm and peaceful.

And quiet.

Dave slipped up behind me. "Kinda amazing, isn't it?"

I turned. "Which part do you mean?"

"Aside from just being alive, not a single trick-or-treater knocked on the door." He looked over with a sly grin and said, "I wonder what this place looked like to them as they worked the street."

We went back inside and cleaned up the salt from the circles. We took it outside, surrounding Dave's duplex with it. Back inside we looked at the clock, realizing it was midnight.

"This gives witching hour a whole new context."

Dave and Stephanie groaned. Then Dave offered a suggestion: "We should go check out Clevis's."

We loaded into my car and drove over to the property. It was dark but not ominous. We couldn't tell if anyone was there, so we kept going. It was quiet as the tomb; we figured the owners weren't real happy at the moment.

But Dave was not quite finished yet: "We should go check out the shotgun house. We can get closer there."

Chapter 25
Stephanie and the Shotgun House Reprise

David

The first truth about awareness is that the world out there is not really like we think it is. We think it is a world of objects but it really isn't. You say you agree with me because everything can be reduced to being a field of energy. But you are merely intuiting a truth. To reason it out is not to verify it. I am not interested in your agreement or disagreement but in your attempt to comprehend what *is* involved in this truth. You cannot witness fields of energy—not as an average man, that is. Now, if you were able to see them you would be a seer, in which case, you would be the one explaining the truths about awareness to me. Conclusions arrived at through thorough reasoning have very little or no influence in altering the course of our lives. This is precisely why we have the countless examples of people who have the clearest convictions, yet act completely opposite of those convictions time and time again. Even sadder, the only explanation for their behavior that they offer up is their humanity. The notion that to err is human. Hogwash!

The first truth is that the world is as it looks; yet it isn't. It's not as solid and real as our perception has been led to believe, but it isn't a mirage, either. The world is not an illusion, or a hologram, as some physicists believe; it's real on the one hand, and unreal on the other. Pay close attention to this, for it must be understood, not just accepted.

We perceive. This is a hard fact. But how we perceive is malleable, because we learn what to perceive. Something out there is affecting our senses. This is the part that is real. The unreal part is what our senses tell us is there. Take a mountain, for instance. Our senses tell us that it is an object. It has size, color, and form. We even have categories of mountains, and they are downright accurate. Now there is nothing wrong with that; the flaw is simply that it has never occurred to us that our senses play only a superficial role. Our senses perceive the way they do because a specific feature of our awareness forces them to do so.

I've used the term *the world* to mean everything that surrounds us. I have a better term, of course, but it would be quite incomprehensible to you. Seers say that we think there is a world of objects out there only because of our awareness. But what's really out there is the Indescribable Force's emanations, fluid, forever in motion, and yet unchanging—eternal. What we do is tap into it and ride it like surfers on the quantum wave.

Robbie

It was dark at the shotgun house. We pulled to the far side of the curve, back by the driveway. The night had taken its toll. I was exhausted. Dave looked a little tuckered out. Stephanie appeared to have aged 10 years.

The weariness strained his voice when Dave spoke. "You kids go have fun; check it out for me. I'm worn out."

I rolled my eyes; Stephanie snickered. We walked toward the front door. It was a quiet night. I would have expected a little more activity on Halloween. We circled the house in silent anticipation. There was no activity. Nothing came jumping out of the shadows. Not even the normal goose bumps. We must have done something right. All was calm and serene. We came around to the back of the house. Everyone in the neighborhood had dogs, yet not a single bark or whine. We were still in an altered state.

As we walked down the driveway, I felt this malevolence grow up strong behind us. I turned around to look into the gaping black maw of the open garage. That was where everything had gone. It was mad.

Stephanie had continued on; she was almost to the street. When she heard me stop, she turned around.

The open door was amazing. It was a moonlit sky and we were in town. There was enough ambient light to clearly see the surroundings. The doorway was different. Whatever light was shining into the garage was extinguished as it crossed the threshold. I was drawn like a moth to the flame. The darkness didn't seem to like that idea.

I took a step toward the garage and got pushed back hard two steps. Then I really wanted to see what was in that garage. I took a step forward; in my mind I surrounded myself with a bubble of white light. This time I didn't get pushed back. I did feel the pressure but it was on the bubble, not me. I couldn't step forward, though. I tried. I was frozen in place!

I stopped for a second taking a deep calming breath. I added more white light to the bubble. I took a small step forward. There was an invisible wall. It kept trying to push me back. I pressed forward one slow step at a time. I added as much chi as I could imagine into the bubble. Then I could take another step.

A noise broke through my concentration. It was rustling in the tall grass throughout the yard. To each side I could see small luminescent shapes. There were glowing orbs starting to gather. Some of them resembled little garden gnomes. In the heightened state I was in, I knew they weren't a problem. They weren't there to cause mischief; they were just drawn to the psychic fireworks. I was aware of some larger entities that had come down from the cemetery. The dead had come to witness.

They didn't matter. Getting in that garage did. I pushed forward, every step an effort. I was going to get there. The little creatures were gathering around, closer and closer, as I advanced on the garage. The last push was the hardest. I felt physical pressure pushing me back. The wild thing was I felt pressure pushing against the picture I was holding in my mind. I was trying to push the bubble into the blackness proper. My light wasn't extinguishing as it entered the threshold. Then came the last step; I was finally there.

"Oh my god! Robbie Run! Run!"

I heard Stephanie spin and go running to the car. The spell broke. The dogs in one of the nearby yards started barking. Immediately, all the dogs in that part of the neighborhood let loose the alarm. I looked one more time at the malignant opening, then turned to join the others at the car. The glowing little green critters scattered before me as I slowly walked toward the others. I got into the car and drove back to Dave's house. Nobody said anything until we got back.

Dave finally asked Stephanie, "What went on? What did you see back there?"

"When I first turned around I saw a big black cloud form out of the garage. Then it flew forward, hitting Robbie square in the chest. It knocked him back pretty good. Then it drew back to hit him again. I wanted to warn him, but I was enthralled. I couldn't yell or look away; all I could do was watch. When the cloud struck out again, a white bubble surrounded Robbie. The cloud bounced off but then started pushing against the bubble again. This time it was a more steady push. The white around Robbie would grow big and move forward, then the black would grow strong and start to envelop the bubble he was in. It just kept pushing back and forth. When he got to the mouth of the garage the black completely surround him. That's when I noticed all the little green entities in the grass that were surrounding him, too. I managed to look to my left. There were several glowing shapes all gathered around. I thought they were getting ready to attack him."

"Well that's enough fun for one night." Dave sighed. "I'm going to walk Stephanie home. We should all get some sleep. Tomorrow's another day; who knows what surprises lay in store for us. I, for one, want to face them well rested."

Aftermath

David

There are three kinds of bad habits that we use over and over when confronted with unusual life situations. First, we may ignore what's happening or what has happened and feel as if it had never occurred. That one is the bigot's way. Second, we may accept everything at its face value and feel as if we know what's going on. That's the pious man's way. Third, we may become obsessed with an event because either we cannot disregard it or we cannot accept it wholeheartedly. That's the fool's way.

There is, however, a fourth way—the correct way, the warrior's way. A warrior acts as if nothing had ever happened, because he doesn't believe in anything, yet he accepts everything at its face value. He accepts without accepting and disregards without disregarding. He never feels as if he truly knows, nor does he feel as if nothing has ever happened. He acts as if he is in control, even though he might be shaking in his boots. To act in such a manner dissipates obsession.

Robbie

"I have to see!"

"What do think you'll see? We didn't actually go there and kick the doors down. It looked pretty quiet when we did a quick drive by last night." Dave chuckled. "Don't you have faith?"

"Oh, I have faith, but I'm just curious to see if there was any physical fallout. I thought we spun up some major mojo. Maybe lightning hit the house. I don't know; I just wanna go see."

As we headed down 2nd Street the laughter died away. We came up to Clevis's place and slowed down. I caught my breath.

Dave stared as we turned the corner. "I have to admit I'm stunned. I don't think I've ever seen anything like that."

It wasn't just Clevis's bungalow; it was all of the buildings on the property. They had become a "before" photo for Sherwin-Williams. The two apartment buildings had been painted a dark, almost forest green. The house had been off-white. All three were now gray. Paint flecks were scattered on the ground as if they just exploded off the buildings. The paint left on the structures was peeled back exposing the wood underneath. We drove away in silence. We had accomplished what we had set out to do. But was it only temporary? Deep down inside, I knew it was. I knew that one day, Dave and I would meet up again, in some lonely swamp or desolate suburban home, to face this thing again. I made it a point there and then to become the best man of knowledge I could ever become.

The doors were now open for me. I can't walk into a theater or any other building or place and not know immediately if it's haunted or not. I have continued on the warrior's path. When I have been ready, the teachers I have needed have appeared in my life. The obstacles that I have needed have also manifested—some like our story here, some more benign. The more I have learned, the more I have learned I know very little.

Maybe it was just a mass hallucination. Was it psychological? Indeed it was to a degree. Were we all somehow feeding into the same fantasy, creating our reality? All I can say is, at the time for the people involved, it was reality. The universe is not as strange and wonderful as we can imagine it. It is far more than we can even begin to conceive.

Penelope had her doors opened; but then they may have only been half shut, anyway. The good news is the nasty things went away, but her experiencing spirits did not. She wasn't harassed, but when lost souls sense you can see them they are drawn to that light. This was not a part of her husband's reality. When he returned from overseas, he immediately had her Baker Acted. In Florida, this means you can be checked in for a psychiatric evaluation with little or no effort. When the doctors realized she was no threat to herself or others, she was released. In fact, she was quite competent. With that behind her, she divorced Norman. She then moved back to Tallahassee to be with her son and parents, and successfully resumed her career.

Dave

This story was difficult for me to work on. The effects of this encounter were long lasting. Over time, many of the details had been blocked out. As a result of this episode, I completely left the arena of the metaphysical, focusing strictly on the scientific study of the paranormal and its effects on the environment as well as people. It wasn't until many years later that Robbie contacted me. We decided to try to piece together the story. Fortunately, Robbie remembered nearly everything. His retelling the story to me, added to the rewrite process of this book, brought back many buried memories from the past. The story is true; the events really occurred. Even if you don't believe it, it's a good tale.

Our Humble Opinion

There is a moral hidden in the pages. We are concerned today with the bumper crop of demonologists that are plying their trade, with little or no formal education in the field. They fancy themselves as real demon hunters based on reading a book, watching a TV show, or just surfing the net. Our concern is that one day they will actually encounter something very real and not be prepared to deal with it. The fact is that there are thousands of "Clevises" out there, all conjuring demons—making deals with the darkness.

Though it seemed like it took years to deal with this, the reality is it took two months. When we began, we did not have a plan, but by walking the path we chose, the plan unfolded itself to us. We were extremely lucky.

However, you cannot undergo an experience like this without a deep and profound effect on your life. We have lived with the reverberations of our fun with Clevis ever since. The resultant backlash, trials, and triumphs of our lives have been touched by our encounter with evil. It has been a wild and crazy adventure, deserving a much deeper exploration and explanation than we have space for here.

David left the path for many years and became an authority on the technology of paranormal investigations. He has only recently started walking the path again. Robbie has never veered from the direction Spirit pointed him in.

Glossary

apparition A ghostlike image of a person.

arachnophobia Fear of spiders and other arachnids such as scorpions.

delusion An impression that is believed despite being contradicted by what is.

demonic Characteristic of demons or evil spirits.

fabrication Manufacturing or creating something.

forbearance Restraint. Tolerant self-control.

hallucination A perception of something not present.

innocuous Not likely to offend.

maelstrom A powerful whirlpool in the sea or a river.

occult Supernatural, mystical, or magical beliefs, practices, or phenomena.

olfactory Relating to the sense of smell.

pagan A person who has nontraditional religious beliefs.

paranormal Phenomena that are beyond the scope of normal scientific understanding.

poltergeist A ghost responsible for physical disturbances.

possessed Controlled by an evil spirit.

preternatural Beyond what is normal or natural.

quantum A quantity of energy proportional in magnitude to the frequency of the radiation it represents.

totem A natural object or animal believed to have spiritual significance and adopted as an emblem.

trickster One who deceives people.

vertigo A sensation of loss of balance.

For More Information

American Society for Psychical Research, Inc. (ASPR)
5 West 73rd Street
New York, NY 10023
(212) 799-5050
Website: http://www.aspr.com

This organization's mission is to explore extraordinary or unexplained phenomena that have been called psychic or paranormal and their implications for our understanding of consciousness, the universe, and the nature of existence. It addresses questions with scientific research and offers educational activities including lectures and conferences.

Ghost Hunters
Syfy Channel
NBCUniversal Cable Entertainment Group
30 Rockefeller Plaza
New York, NY 10112
(212) 664-4444
Website: http://www.syfy.com/ghosthunters

In each episode of the television program *Ghost Hunters*, Jason Hawes and his team of paranormal investigators, TAPS (the Atlantic Paranormal Society) investigate paranormal activity across the country.

Parapsychological Association, Inc. (PA)
P.O. Box 24173
Columbus, OH 43224
(202) 318-2364
Website: www.parapsych.org

The Parapsychological Association is the international professional organization of scientists and scholars engaged in the study of "psi" (or "psychic") experiences, such as telepathy, clairvoyance, and psychic healing. The PA endorses no ideologies or beliefs other than the value of rigorous scientific and scholarly inquiry.

TAPS ParaMagazine
P.O. Box 233
Fly Creek, NY 13337
Email: jvj@tapsparamag.com
Website: www.tapsparamag.com

Founded by the Atlantic Paranormal Society (TAPS) in 2008, *ParaMagazine* is America's premiere paranormal print and digital publication featuring the top minds on the topics of paranormal investigations, cryptozoology, ufology, and spiritual beliefs.

Websites

Because of the changing nature of Internet links, Rosen Publishing has developed an online list of websites related to the subject of this book. This site is updated regularly. Please use this link to access the list:

http://www.rosenlinks.com/HH/exor

For Further Reading

Botz, Corinne May. *Haunted Houses*. New York, NY: Monacelli, 2010.

Diehl, Daniel, and Mark Donnelly. *Haunted Houses: Guide to Spooky, Creepy, and Strange Places across the USA*. Mechanicsburg, PA: Stackpole, 2010.

Gibson, Marley, Patrick Burns, and Dave Schrader. *The Other Side: A Teen's Guide to Ghost Hunting and the Paranormal*. Boston, MA: Houghton Mifflin Harcourt, 2009.

Horn, Stacy. *Unbelievable: Investigations into Ghosts, Poltergeists, Telepathy, and Other Unseen Phenomena from the Duke Parapsychology Laboratory*. New York, NY: Ecco, 2009.

Krulos, Tea. *Monster Hunters: On the Trail with Ghost Hunters, Bigfooters, Ufologists, and Other Paranormal Investigators.* Chicago, IL: Chicago Review, 2015.

Lynch, Gordon J., Diane Canwell, and Jonathan Sutherland. *Famous Ghosts and Haunted Places* (The Supernatural). New York, NY: Rosen Publishing, 2012.

Peck, M. Scott. *Glimpses of the Devil: A Psychiatrist's Personal Accounts of Possession, Exorcism, and Redemption*. New York, NY: Free Press, 2009.

Sagan, Carl. *The Demon-Haunted World: Science as a Candle in the Dark*. New York, NY: Ballantine, 2008.

Southall, Richard. *Haunted Route 66: Ghosts of America's Legendary Highway*. Woodbury, MN: Llewellyn Worldwide, 2013.

Teitelbaum, Michael. *Ghosts: And Real-Life Ghost Hunters*. New York, NY: Franklin Watts, 2008.

Thompson, Dave. *Haunted America FAQ: All That's Left to Know about the Most Haunted Houses, Cemeteries, Battlefields, and More*. Montclair, NJ: Backbeat, 2015.

Zepke, Terrance. *A Ghost Hunter's Guide to the Most Haunted Houses in America*. Chicago, IL: Safari, 2013.

Index

T

V

W

About the Authors

Robbie Lunt

Robbie is an arcanologist, certified entertainment electrician, and certified technology specialist currently residing in Washoe Valley, Nevada. He is a proud member of the Way of Nature Fellowship. He has had more than 20 years of doing energy work in both Tai Chi and Reiki. When he's not doing research or haunting a theatre, if you search hard enough, you might find him kayaking or skiing in the Sierra Nevadas.

David Rountree

David is a duality, forging ahead to discover scientific explanations for the metaphysical in the physical, balancing the path of a scientist with the path of the shaman, and uniting two worlds under a single philosophy. When he is not designing some apparatus to measure the unknown, he can be found wandering on a mountain or along a stream speaking with animals in any wilderness less frequented by human beings.